UNDERSTANDING
INTELLIGENT DESIGN

WILLIAM A. DEMBSKI
SEAN McDOWELL

HARVEST HOUSE PUBLISHERS

EUGENE, OREGON

Cover by Abris, Veneta, Oregon

Cover photo © Kasia Biel / iStockphoto

Back cover author photo © Laszlo Bencze

This work published in association with the Conversant Media Group, P.O. Box 3006, Redmond, WA, 98007.

ConversantLife.com is a trademark of Conversant Media Group. Harvest House Publishers, Inc., is a licensee of the trademark ConversantLife.com.

UNDERSTANDING INTELLIGENT DESIGN
Copyright © 2008 by William A. Dembski and Sean McDowell
Published by Harvest House Publishers
Eugene, Oregon 97402
www.harvesthousepublishers.com

Library of Congress Cataloging-in-Publication Data

Dembski, William A., 1960-
Understanding intelligent design / William A. Dembski and Sean McDowell.
    p. cm.
Includes bibliographical references.
ISBN 978-0-7369-2442-9
1. Intelligent design (Teleology) 2. Creationism. 3. Evolution (Biology)—Religious aspects—Christianity.
I. McDowell, Sean. II. Title.
BS651.D455 2008
213—dc22

2008014216

Printed in the United States of America

14 15 16 / VP-NI / 10 9 8 7

Download a Deeper Experience

Sean McDowell is part of a faith-based online community called ConversantLife.com. At this website, people engage their faith in entertainment, creative arts, science and technology, global concerns, and other culturally relevant topics. While you're reading this book, or after you have finished reading, go to www.conversantlife.com /seanmcdowell and use these icons to read and download additional material from Sean that is related to this book:

Resources: Download study guide materials for personal devotions or a small-group Bible study.

Videos: Click on this icon for interviews with Bill Dembski and Sean and video clips on various topics.

Blogs: Read through Sean's blogs and articles and comment on them.

Podcasts: Stream ConversantLife.com podcasts and audio clips from Sean.

conversant life .com

engage your faith

To Ben Stein,
for his courage to stand for freedom
of inquiry and expression
in the documentary
Expelled

Acknowledgments

We would like to thank Mark Matlock for encouraging us to work together on this project as well as Joel Borofsky for first broaching this project with Mark. We appreciate the insightful and thorough editing of Carlos Delgado and Denyse O'Leary. Stan Jantz, thanks for believing in this project and for the vision and passion you bring to ConversantLife.com. Terry Glaspey, thanks for getting the ball rolling with Harvest House and for your constant support.

I (Bill) want to thank my wife, Jana, for the love and humor she brings to our family. I also want to thank Grant Kaul for first putting the bug in my ear about writing a user-friendly book on intelligent design that tells readers, in plain language, what it is, why it's important, and what they can do about it.

I (Sean) would like to thank my mom, Dottie, and my wife, Stephanie, for their encouragement and support throughout the research and writing process.

Contents

FOREWORD
BY JOSH MCDOWELL

The origin and order of the universe. It's hard to imagine a greater question or one more hotly debated through the ages. The biblical writers boldly proclaim that the world is not an accident but is the creation of a personal God. In Psalm 19:1-2 (NLT), David says, "The heavens proclaim the glory of God. The skies display his craftsmanship. Day after day they continue to speak; night after night they make him known." Writing nearly 1000 years before Christ, David declared that nature reveals knowledge about God. And in Romans 1, Paul says that creation reveals invisible attributes of God, such as His power and divine nature. Believers should not be surprised that scientists have recently begun to find remarkable evidence of design in the natural world.

The intelligent design (ID) movement has made waves not only in the scientific community but also in the culture at large. Influential newspapers such as the *New York Times* and *USA Today* have discussed developments in ID and how it relates to education. The major motion picture *Expelled: No Intelligence Allowed* was released featuring Ben Stein. Magazines such as *US News & World Report*, *Time*, and *Newsweek* have featured intelligent-design stories on their front covers. Movies and television shows frequently address the issue of Darwinism and intelligent design. In fact, during the presidential debates, Republican candidates were asked if they believed in evolution. The debate shows no signs of slowing down. More than ever, Christians—and non-Christians—need to be accurately informed about this crucial issue.

In my interactions with Christians, I have found that many of them are not quite sure what to think about ID, let alone able to understand what it really means. Many are aware of the remarkable evidence for design coming from scientists working in diverse fields such as neuroscience, biology, chemistry, physics, and cosmology, but they fail to see how it relates to their lives today. As Bill and Sean so clearly demonstrate in *Understanding Intelligent Design,* the fingerprint of God can be seen from the smallest cell to the farthest reaches of the universe.

On the other hand, many creationists are hesitant about embracing the ID movement because some of the leading scientists of the movement do not specifically identify the designer (at least not in their professional work). I can appreciate this concern, but I believe there may be a more fruitful way of approaching this issue.

For much of my life I have defended the historical resurrection of Jesus, the deity of Christ, and the reliability of the Scriptures. After a lifetime of study, I am ever more convinced that the Bible is an accurate rendition of history that has powerful personal application for my life today, even in the twenty-first century. To make the strongest case for the Scriptures possible, I often look to the field of archaeology. Many findings of the past few decades have shed incredible new light on the world of the ancient Near East during the time of Christ. With each new find my confidence in the Bible grows. Regardless of the religious conviction of the archaeologist, the findings can still be used to support the biblical description of history. Some of the most significant archaeological finds owe to non-Christians.

As my friend Kerby Anderson has pointed out, we ought to think of scientists working on intelligent design in the same way. Intelligent design is a scientific field of study that looks to recognize evidence for design in the natural world. Some of the scientists working on intelligent design are Christians, but many are not. Even so, they are finding signs of intelligence in nature that support the biblical picture of creation. And their research—as you will see in this book—is truly mind-boggling! Just because some scientists may not be Christians doesn't mean we can't benefit from their work. We can evaluate their research and see if the God of the Bible best fits the evidence of science.

Personally speaking, I have found *Understanding Intelligent Design* to be a powerful witness to creation. Although I have read Psalm 19:1-2 many times in my life, the findings in this volume gave me confidence in its truth like never before. What excites me most about this volume is that Bill and Sean have simplified very sophisticated ideas for people (like you and me!) who are intrigued by the debate but may not be trained in the natural sciences. *Understanding Intelligent Design* makes the revolutionary findings in science interesting, relevant, and accessible. It's a must-read.

In fact, my hope is that many people, and in particular *young* people, will get a copy of this volume, study it, and share the ideas with others. Intelligent design proponents are on to something big—*very* big. This is evident by the increasingly intense rhetoric surrounding this issue today. A recent cover of *Time* magazine captured the debate perfectly. It was boldly entitled, "Evolution Wars." In a clear parody of the Sistine Chapel, the gray-haired figure of God reaches down toward the brow of a chimpanzee, who is pondering the subtitle: "The push to teach 'intelligent design' raises a question: Does God have a place in science class?"[1]

From my perspective, the reason evolution is so hotly debated is quite simple: Evolution raises fundamental questions about what it means to be human. Are we accidental by-products of blind forces in nature? Or are we the pinnacle of creation intended by a personal and loving God? Can all the beauty, complexity, and diversity of life be explained by random variation and natural selection? Or is the natural world best explained as the workings of a designer? It's difficult to imagine a series of questions more important than these.

More than ever, there is a need for a book that takes the revolutionary findings in science and makes them understandable to the person on the street. That is why *Understanding Intelligent Design* is so timely. While the rhetoric in the God-debate is heating up, Bill and Sean make a solid case for design in the universe, respectfully engaging those with whom they disagree. Altogether, I found this an enjoyable, eye-opening, and fascinating read. Whether you are a skeptic, seeker, or believer, this book will challenge you. I highly recommend it.

Josh McDowell

Welcome to the Debate

As the lunch bell rang in our ears, Mike slipped sheepishly into my classroom, slouched into a seat, folded his arms on the desk, and buried his face in them. I knew he wouldn't want anyone around when he came to talk to me; he didn't want to seem uncool in front of his friends. But what did he want to talk about? Grades? Girls? The basketball coach? As I approached, he sat up, looked me in the eyes, and blurted, "Mr. McDowell, we need to talk. I think I'm losing my faith."

Like many people, Mike was caught up in his day-to-day routine, and he didn't usually think much about his Christian beliefs. So why now? Well, the night before, he had come across an atheist website that raised many questions he had never considered. Lacking the intellectual tools and confidence to answer the challenges, he began to question his faith.

Yes, he now had many questions to ask me about the Bible and Jesus, but his deepest concerns were about something else—the origin of mankind. Is evolution true? Does evolution do away with God? Did God use evolution to create humans? Is there any scientific evidence that life is designed?

I'm thankful Mike trusted me enough to enlist my help with this challenge to his faith. Over the next few months, we spent many lunch hours exploring crucial apologetics questions, focusing mainly on the scientific evidence for design in biology, physics, and biochemistry. He later shared with me that had I not been there, he likely would have lost his faith.

Studies reveal that for today's youth, Mike's experience is common. When interviewed for the 2005 National Study of Youth and Religion, thousands of teenagers who had been raised in religious homes said that over time, their faith slackened and they became "non-religious." Why?

When asked to explain their loss of faith, their most common answer (32 percent) was intellectual skepticism. Specific answers included these: "Some stuff was too far-fetched for me to believe in." "I think *scientifically* there is no proof." "There were too many questions that can't be answered."[1] Clearly, then, responsible discipleship today requires knowing the scientific evidence for an intelligent designer.

Roughly 30 years ago, in 1980, I (Bill) had a similar experience—one which over the years has motivated my work on intelligent design. Sadly, it ended quite differently from Sean's experience with Mike. When I was a college student, I met two young men in their early twenties on the streets of Chicago. I had become a Christian a year before and was enthusiastic about sharing my faith. Our conversation soon turned to the claims of Christ. I described what Jesus meant to me and what I thought Jesus should mean to them. Having had a bit too much to drink, they began to mock me. But then something strange happened—they broke down in tears.

It turned out that these men were graduates of Wheaton College, one of the finest evangelical Christian colleges in the country. They were now students at one of the mainline seminaries near the University of Chicago. Through their studies at seminary, they lost their faith. In tears, they kept repeating, "We wish we could believe the way you do, but we can't anymore."

What happened to their faith? Presumably, Wheaton ought to have prepared them for any challenges to the faith that they might have encountered. Yet at seminary their faith rapidly disintegrated. Since that encounter with these two young men, I have been through the educational curriculum at Princeton Theological Seminary, also a mainline seminary. I can attest that students at a seminary like theirs (and at most public universities) get two things that can irreparably shatter their faith.

First, they are taught that the Bible is a hodgepodge of ancient texts written by rubes who didn't know half of what they were talking about and certainly weren't inspired by God. The Bible's reliability and authority are thus systematically undermined. It is approached less as a sacred text than as a patchwork of writings by people out of touch with reality.

A second, closely related problem is that students are taught a way of looking at the world known as *naturalism*. Naturalism sees the world as a self-contained system of matter and energy that operates by unbroken natural laws. According to naturalism, everything in the world happens by chance and necessity. God may or may not exist, but nature operates without reference to Him and it shows no sign of His presence.

How does naturalism relate to Christianity? Clearly, if naturalism is true, then Christianity is false. If God cannot act in the natural world, then Jesus cannot be divine, the miracles attributed to Him must have natural explanations, and the Bible is not the inspired Word of God. All the order and complexity in the world is then the result of a blind, material process, not God's decision to create.

Young people are indoctrinated into naturalism in grade school, high school, and then college. Sometimes they are also indoctrinated in churches, as on Evolution Weekend, when some congregations celebrate Darwin's birthday.[2] The most effective tool for promoting naturalism is Darwinian evolution, or Darwinism for short. Darwinism teaches that all life is descended from a common ancestor (you and your pet snail are cousins) by a process of undirected changes in genes that get sifted by natural selection. Natural selection is Darwin's substitute for God.

Christians of all ages hear this propaganda. Moreover, they face enormous cultural pressure to refrain from questioning it.

Consequently, over time, many come to believe that blind material forces are sufficient to account for all the design, order, and complexity of the world. Something like that probably happened to those two young men in Chicago. It has happened to many others, including prominent advocates of atheism and Darwinism, such as Michael Shermer and E.O. Wilson.

EVANGELICAL CHRISTIAN YESTERDAY, ARDENT DARWINIST TODAY!

According to Michael Shermer, a columnist for *Scientific American* and founding publisher of *Skeptic* magazine,

> I had found the One True Religion, and it was my duty—indeed it was my pleasure—to tell others about it, including my parents, brothers and sisters, friends, and even total strangers. In other words, I "witnessed" to people—a polite term for trying to convert them (one wag called it Amway with Bibles). Of course, I read the Bible, as well as books about the Bible. I regularly attended youth church groups, one in particular at a place called "The Barn," a large red house in La Crescenta, California, at which Christians gathered a couple of times a week to sing, pray, and worship. I got so involved that I eventually began to put on Bible study courses myself.[3]

But as Shermer continues the story elsewhere,

> By the end of my first year in a graduate program in experimental psychology at California State University, Fullerton, I had abandoned Christianity and stripped off my silver ichthus, replacing what was for me the stultifying dogma of a 2,000-year-old religion with the worldview of an always changing, always fresh science. The passionate nature of this perspective was espoused most emphatically by my evolutionary biology professor.[4]

And E.O. Wilson, author of *Consilience* and *Dear Pastor,* writes,

> When I was fifteen, I entered the Southern Baptist Church with

great fervor and interest in the fundamentalist religion. I left at seventeen when I got to the University of Alabama and heard about evolutionary theory.[5]

Shermer and Wilson are hardly unique. A recent study polled 149 eminent evolutionists and found that 78 percent were pure naturalists (no God), and only two were clearly theists (traditional idea of God). The rest were agnostics or deists. The deists believe some sort of divinity might have got things rolling, but it is not God in any sense that Christians understand.[6]

So here's the big question: Are all these people losing their faith because evolution proves that God is a fairytale? Let's find out!

The Great Worldview Conflict

Mike's experience was not isolated or accidental. It is part of a larger picture, a cultural conflict raging all around us. This conflict practically defines the twenty-first century, and it makes a huge difference to all of our lives. Here is how Robert Reich, former Secretary of Labor in the Clinton Administration, now a professor at Brandeis University, understands that conflict:

> The great conflict of the twenty-first century may be between the West and terrorism. But terrorism is a tactic, not a belief. The underlying battle will be between modern civilization and anti-modernist fanatics; between those who believe in the primacy of the individual and those who believe that human beings owe blind allegiance to a higher authority; between those who give priority to life in this world and those who believe that human life is no more than preparation for an existence beyond life; between those who believe that truth is revealed solely through scripture and religious dogma, and those who rely primarily on science, reason, and logic.[7]

Reich here mistakenly regards science and religion as at war (we discuss their relationship in chapter 5). Moreover, he is clearly pushing an agenda when he describes modern civilization as inherently secular and atheistic. (The vast majority of Americans, who presumably belong to and have a stake in "modern civilization," are theists).

Still, Reich is on to something in underscoring that the conflict here is between competing ways of looking at the world: the view that blind material forces are sufficient to account for all the order and complexity of the world versus the view that a designing intelligence best accounts for them. The first view is naturalism. The second, held by Christians, Jews, and Muslims, is theism.

A way of looking at the world is called a *worldview.* In her book *Total Truth,* Nancy Pearcey defines a worldview as a mental map of reality. Just as an accurate physical map gets us to our destination, an accurate worldview gets our lives on track. Everyone has a worldview whether one realizes it or not and even if one cannot clearly explain it. All the big decisions in life flow from one's worldview.

Worldviews answer three fundamental questions:

- *Origin:* How did it all begin? Where did we come from?
- *Predicament:* What went wrong? What is the source of evil and suffering?
- *Resolution:* What can be done about it? How can the world be set aright?[8]

The Christian Worldview

According to the Christian worldview, God freely created the world. The Bible opens with Genesis 1:1: "In the beginning God created…" It is no accident that the first thing the Bible teaches is creation. Creation implies purpose. Because we are created, there is a purpose for our existence, for the family, for work, for sex, and for how we ought to live. Creation by a loving God is our *origin.*

Freedom comes from knowing our purpose and living consistently with it. The Westminster Catechism tells us that our chief end (our purpose) is to know God and enjoy Him forever. In the fall, however, humans rebelled against God and brought evil into the world—not just personal evil, but natural evil that has corrupted all of God's creation. That is our *predicament.*

Redemption is found in Jesus Christ. In Jesus, God becomes human, takes the sin of the world on Himself at the cross, and in His resurrection restores the life of the world. One day the world will recover its original truth, goodness, and beauty, and we will be united with God, able to see Him face-to-face. That is the *resolution* to our predicament.

The Naturalistic Worldview

The world according to naturalism looks quite different. Humans, in this view, are not the crown of creation, the carefully designed outcome of a purposeful creator. Certainly they are not creatures made in the image of a benevolent God. In *Ever Since Darwin,* Stephen J. Gould wrote, "Biology took away our status as paragons created in the image of God."[9] Humans are merely an accident of natural history, the result of the mindless process of evolution. We are the result of a world that creates itself. This is our *origin.*

Within a naturalistic worldview, our problems with evil and suffering could not stem from a rebellion against God because God does not exist and therefore plays no role in the universe. Rather, evil is a natural consequence of the inherently clumsy and opportunistic process of evolution. As evolution bumbles along, our genes get messed up, and our environment shapes us to be competitive, selfish, and cruel. As a result, we are ridden with cognitive, emotional, and physical disorders. This is our *predicament.*

Many naturalists readily agree that Jesus Christ was a great moral figure, but they reject that through His cross and resurrection He redeemed humanity. No, we must redeem ourselves by the advances of science, technology, therapy, and drugs. In other words, we must solve our own problems and do so without recourse to anything beyond the physical world. That is the *resolution* to our predicament.

Naturalism's vision of the future is bleak. The sun will one day burn up the earth or burn out completely. With its passing, all our hopes and aspirations will likewise pass away. In the end, we will perish, leaving no trace and no memory. Charles Darwin struggled with this in his autobiography:

> The view now held by most physicists [is] that the sun with all the planets will in time grow too cold for life, unless indeed some great body dashes into the sun and thus give it fresh life...Believing as I do that man in the distant future will be a far more perfect creature than he is now, it is an intolerable thought that he and all other sentient beings are doomed to complete annihilation after such long-continued slow progress.[10]

Other worldviews exist besides Christianity and naturalism. Buddhists, for example, believe that attachment to one's own existence and to anything else in the universe is the cause of suffering and that detachment is the cure. In this book, however, we focus on the conflict between naturalism and theism and specifically between Darwinian naturalism (naturalism as justified by Darwinism) and Christian theism (theism as understood by Christians). That is the key conflict in our society right now.

Darwinism: the Universal Acid

Darwin's theory of evolution, often referred to as Darwinism, inspires the best-known form of naturalism. In *Darwin's Dangerous Idea*, philosopher Daniel Dennett says that every aspect of human life—including education, relationships, and politics—must be understood in light of Darwinian evolution. Dennett wants *all* reality to be understood within a Darwinian framework. Why? Because

Darwinism tells us our creation story, and such a story always controls how we interpret reality. If Darwinism is true, then Dennett is correct: All aspects of reality should be understood within this light.

Given how widely Darwinism is accepted, we should not be surprised that virtually every field of study is now being "Darwinized." Every subject is supposedly to be understood in the light of Darwin's theory of evolution. Consider just a few examples of recent books and the disciplines they are aiming to transform:

- *Why We Get Sick: The New Science of Darwinian Medicine* by Randolph M. Nesse and George C. Williams
- *Economics as an Evolutionary Science* by Arthur Gandolfi and Anna Gandolfi
- *Evolutionary Jurisprudence* by John H. Beckstrom
- *Religion Explained: The Evolutionary Origins of Religious Thought* by Pascal Boyer
- *Literary Darwinism: Evolution, Human Nature, and Literature* by Joseph Carroll
- *Darwinizing Culture* by Robert Aunger (ed.)

Darwinism is one of the few subjects that popular culture holds in awe. It is often treated as the pinnacle of science (an honor that we'll soon see is undeserved). For example, in a *Friends* episode, Phoebe and Ross discuss the merits of Darwinian evolution. Shocked to find that Phoebe rejects it, Ross says, "Uh, excuse me. Evolution is not for you to buy, Phoebe. Evolution is scientific fact, like, like, like the air we breathe, like gravity."

Darwinism even shows up in the children's movie *Lilo & Stitch*. In one scene, Pleakley instructs the Grand Councilwoman that earth is a protected planet, and therefore she can't destroy it. Pleakley denies that there is intelligent life on earth. But he does say that it is inhabited by "primitive humanoid life forms" and that "every time an asteroid strikes their planet, they have to begin life all over." During this discussion, the Grand Councilwoman sees a picture of an amoeba evolving into a fish, a lizard, and so on until the emergence of man. What is the underlying assumption here? That evolution routinely happens after each asteroid hit. No further explanation is offered, none is expected.

We see another example of pop-culture Darwinism in a recent episode of *The Family Guy*. One of the characters, Peter, tells the evolutionary story of the universe from the Big Bang to the very first dinosaurs. Then, according to Kansas state law, he must present the church's alternative to the theory of evolution. So out of the water comes a genie who causes a car, a deer, a bear, Santa Claus, and other objects to magically materialize. The take-home lesson is that either you accept evolution (which today means Darwinism) or you believe something completely ridiculous (like things just popping into existence by magic).

Are supporters of Darwinism giving us a fair picture here? Is it just plain silly to deny Darwinism? What if there is a better explanation for the origin and structure of the universe than Darwinian naturalism? What if the world has been designed for a particular purpose? If so, the attempt to understand all reality within a Darwinian perspective would be a colossal mistake.

Challenging Darwinism

Why is it so important to challenge Darwinism? The problem isn't just that Darwinism is false—lots of things are false that nobody worries about. The problem is that Darwinism is no longer merely a scientific theory, but an *ideology*. An ideology is an all-encompassing worldview that attempts to explain everything, often on the basis of a single principle (such as natural selection). Moreover, it demands complete obedience from our hearts and minds.

Marxism and fascism were ideologies in this sense, and Darwinism has now become one. In his recent book *What's So Great*

About Christianity, Dinesh D'Souza points out that "we have Darwinism but not Keplerism; we encounter Darwinists but no one describes himself as an Einsteinian. Darwinism has become an ideology."[11]

Darwin attempted to explain how new species, including humans, come into existence. But his theory is now supposed to explain not only the diversity and complexity of life but just about everything else as well. This is how David Berlinski put it in the March 2003 issue of *Commentary:*

> The term "Darwinism" conveys the suggestion of a secular ideology, a global system of belief. So it does and so it surely is. Darwin's theory has been variously used—by Darwinian biologists—to explain the development of bipedal gait, the tendency to laugh when amused, obesity, anorexia nervosa, business negotiations, a preference for tropical landscapes, the evolutionary roots of political rhetoric, maternal love, infanticide, clan formation, marriage, divorce, certain comical sounds, funeral rites, the formation of regular verb forms, altruism, homosexuality, feminism, greed, romantic love, jealousy, warfare, monogamy, polygamy, adultery, the fact that men are pigs, recursion, sexual display, abstract art, and religious beliefs of every description.[12]

This passage would be funnier still if Darwin's loyal followers weren't so deadly earnest. For instance, in *Darwin's Dangerous Idea,* Daniel Dennett suggests that religious believers who talk their children out of believing Darwinian evolution should be caged in zoos or quarantined because they pose a serious threat to the social order.[13] Similarly, the Council of Europe has identified intelligent design theory as a threat to human rights.[14] But the only danger here is to Darwinists who might lose their monopoly on the thoughts and education of society. A free society is free to challenge Darwinism.

Doubting Darwinism

For half a century, Antony Flew was the world's most famous intellectual atheist. Other atheists, such as dictators of communist regimes, may have appeared more often in newspapers, but Flew set the intellectual agenda for modern atheism. His famous lecture "Theology and Falsification," which he personally delivered to C.S. Lewis's Socratic Club, was the most widely reprinted philosophical article in the last five decades. In it, he argued that atheism is the default position and that the burden of proof rests on theists to show that God exists. He went on to write many more books and give many more important lectures.

Then in 2004, he made a shocking announcement: God must exist. In a headline-making reversal, Flew now holds that the universe must be the work of an intelligent designer.

What convinced him to change his mind? Our DNA. "What I think the DNA material has done," remarked Flew, "is show that intelligence must have been involved in getting these extraordinarily diverse elements together...The enormous complexity by which the results were achieved looks to me like the work of intelligence."[15] In an interview for *Philosophia Christi,* he added, "It now seems to me that the findings of more than fifty years of DNA research have provided materials for a new and enormously powerful argument to design."[16]

Why does Flew now believe in God? "The short answer," writes Flew, "is the world picture, as I see it, that has emerged from modern science."[17] Bear in mind that Flew did not have a mystical religious experience. Nor did he become a Christian. Scientific evidence persuaded him that God exists. This evidence, from DNA, did not even exist when he first started arguing for atheism decades earlier.

More and more scientists agree with Antony Flew: The world *appears* designed because it *is* designed. They argue that the design in the world is just as real as the design in a computer chip, a car, or a sports stadium.[18] These scientists have also observed another surprising thing: The hard empirical evidence for Darwinism is in fact quite limited.

Darwin's mechanism of natural selection acting on random variations can account for small-scale changes in living forms: insects developing insecticide resistance, finch populations exhibiting bigger beaks during droughts, and other minor biological adaptations (changes). But neither Darwin's mechanism nor any other purely natural mechanism explains how insects and birds came to exist in the first place. The theory is supposed to explain such large-scale adaptations, but it doesn't.

The Burden of Proof

A few years back, skeptic Michael Shermer wrote a book called *How We Believe*. For it he commissioned a poll of thousands of people. He asked participants why other people believe in God. The most popular answers focused on religious benefits: God comforts us, provides the basis for living a moral life, gives purpose to our lives, and is the source of meaningful religious experiences.

Then Shermer asked participants why they personally believe in God. The number one answer changed drastically. The most common response was the design and complexity of the world. Our natural tendency, it would seem, is to believe the world was designed.

Many Darwinists concede this point. On the first page of his book *The Blind Watchmaker: Why the Evidence of Evolution Reveals a World Without Design*, Richard Dawkins wrote, "Biology is the study of complicated things that give the appearance of having been designed for a purpose."[19] He then spends 350 pages to show why it is only an appearance of design. In *What Mad Pursuit*, Nobel laureate Francis Crick, codiscoverer of the structure of DNA, wrote, "Biologists must constantly keep in mind that what they see was not designed, but rather, evolved."[20]

Here then is a question worth pondering: If a creature looks like a dog, smells like a dog, barks like a dog, feels like a dog, and pants like a dog, doesn't the burden of proof lie with the person who insists the creature isn't a dog? Generally speaking, the burden of proof lies with those who deny our natural intuitions about the world.

That the world bears the marks of design is a basic intuition found throughout history in virtually all cultures. Given such powerful design intuitions, it seems only reasonable that the burden of proof is on those who reject design. Still, as strong as our design intuitions may be, they are not by themselves enough to help young people withstand the pressure in our culture from Darwinian naturalism. We saw this earlier in the cases of Mike and the two young men from Chicago. Therefore we cannot rely only on intuition. We must also advance a scientific case for design.

The Evidence for Design

In media reports, one often hears the following sound bite describing intelligent design: "Life is too complicated to have arisen by natural forces, so it must have been designed." Even though this sound bite may seem intuitively appealing, it is too simplistic for scientific purposes. Do we have a more rigorous way to identify when a system has been intelligently designed?

Intelligent design places our natural design intuitions on a firm foundation of scientific reason and evidence. Intelligent design's main claim is this: Nature exhibits patterns that are best explained as the products of an intelligent cause (design) rather than an undirected material process (chance and necessity). If you think about it, determining whether something is designed ("drawing a design inference") is a necessary part of life. When archaeologists find an oddly shaped rock, they have two basic options: Is it a tool or arrowhead (design)? Or is it merely an odd-shaped chunk of rock (chance and necessity)? Similarly, ripple marks in the sand can be explained by the random motion of waves, whereas "John loves Mary" drawn in the sand clearly indicates design.

The design inferences we make every day can be applied to the biological world. For example, consider the bacterial flagellum (which we will discuss in more detail in chapter 8). In public lectures, Harvard biologist Howard Berg calls the bacterial flagellum "the most efficient machine in the universe." The flagellum is a tiny bidirectional motor-driven propeller on the back of certain bacteria. It spins at tens of thousands of revolutions per minute, can change direction in a quarter of a turn, and propels a bacterium through its watery surroundings. It is a molecular machine. The flagellum has multiple parts that are functionally integrated (like the parts in a watch), so the removal of key parts destroys the function of the entire system.

How did this little motor come about? Darwinists have proposed various explanations. All such explanations try to make plausible how systems simpler than the flagellum might have evolved into a flagellum. But systems simpler than a flagellum don't work as a flagellum, so if they evolved into a flagellum, they must have started off doing something else. But what?

At this point, Darwinists speculate wildly about what those previous systems (known as precursors or intermediates) might have been. But such "arguments from imagination" are not evidence. Undirected material processes give no evidence of producing such complex machinelike structures. But intelligence can and does.

But Wasn't Intelligent Design Defeated at Dover?

Intelligent design has become such a political issue that many people are not even interested in hearing the science arguments. Often, such people will say ID was defeated at Dover. They are referring to the 2005 *Kitzmiller v. Dover* case, in which Judge John E. Jones III concluded "that ID is an interesting theological argument, but that it is not science."[21]

Applauding this ruling, *Time* magazine heralded Jones as one of the 100 most influential people in the world for 2006. And yet evidence for design had convinced Antony Flew, who by any objective standard had been far more influential for not just one year but for five decades.

Here's a little background to the Dover case. In that public school district, teachers were required to read a four-paragraph statement to students, informing them that intelligent design is an alternative theory to Darwinian evolution and that if they were interested, they could read about intelligent design by going to the school library and picking up a book titled *Of Pandas and People*.[22] Many intelligent design advocates, including Seattle's Discovery Institute, the leading ID think tank, did not endorse the compulsory reading of that statement. Also, many teachers who are sympathetic to design consider such a statement to be a poor educational practice. If a topic is that important, teachers should not just direct students to a book about it, but teach it properly.

In his decision, which he delivered in December 20, 2005, Judge Jones made numerous incorrect statements about ID.[23] For example, he falsely claimed that design theorists have published no articles on ID in peer-reviewed scientific journals. Actually, such articles existed at the time, and Judge Jones knew of them.[24] For these reasons and many more, the authors of *Traipsing into Evolution* (a book about the Dover case) conclude, "When cross-checked against the evidence and arguments presented in the court record, many of Judge Jones' key assertions turn out to be erroneous, contradictory, or irrelevant."[25]

Jones's main distinction before being appointed a federal judge was to serve as chairman of the Pennsylvania Liquor Control Board. As neither a scientist nor a scholar, he was ill-equipped to preside over this case. It won't be the last on intelligent design.

Why Is Intelligent Design So Important?

I (Sean) often use the following exercise to help my students reflect on what they believe and why. To begin, I ask them to write down all the reasons people believe what they do. Typically, students give lots of reasons—parents, tradition, Scripture, friends, media, comfort, science, consistency, and so on.

After compiling an extensive list, I then ask which of the reasons for belief are actually valid. In other words, Why *should* you believe something? After we probe each answer, it becomes clear that reasons such as "what makes me happy" (psychological), "the people I like" (sociological), and "my church teaches this" (religious) are not enough. Parents, teachers, friends, religious books, and entire cultures can be mistaken. Comforting beliefs can be false and sometimes even harmful. Scripture and religious authorities are worth believing only if their teachings are true.

As a result of this exercise, most students realize that many of their core beliefs have not been formed by weighing the merits of various options and thereby coming to the most reasonable conclusion. They're not alone. We are all, at times, guilty of faulty thinking. We let ourselves be persuaded for emotional and self-serving reasons rather than by an unbiased examination of the evidence.

This brings us to the main point of this section and the key point of this chapter: *Intelligent design is so important because the evidence for it is compelling, but Darwinists suppress that evidence to promote a naturalistic worldview.* People left to themselves believe that the world is designed. Darwinian propagandists then come along and tell them that Darwin's theory has done away with the need for design (and if there is no design, there is no God). But in fact the evidence is against Darwin's theory. Intelligent design lays out that evidence and presents an exciting scientific alternative to it. In the following chapters, we will explain how this is so.

INTELLIGENT DESIGN
TO THE RESCUE!

SO MANY PEOPLE WERE TALKING ABOUT the BBC series *Planet Earth* that my (Sean's) family decided to purchase the DVDs to see why all the commotion. We were completely blown away! The nature footage they captured is absolutely amazing. Our four-year-old son, Scottie, would ask, "Can we watch *Planet Earth* tonight?"

In my favorite scene, a gigantic great white shark chases a seal. Sharks are swift and powerful; the seal is more agile. But despite its agility, the seal cannot escape earth's most feared predator. The chase ends when the shark explodes from the water and catches the seal in its jaws in midair. The slow-motion footage was worth the price of the entire series. *Incredible!*

But as my wife and I reflected on what we had seen, we felt that something was missing. The series celebrated the powerful forces of nature, but it never mentioned creation. This was so different from the psalmist's worldview: "When I consider your heavens, the work of your fingers, the moon and the stars, which you have set in place, what is man that you are mindful of him, the son of man that you care for him?" (Psalm 8:3-4 NIV).

As fascinating as *Planet Earth* is, viewers are left with the impression that the natural world operates completely on its own, independent of the design or care of a creator. Is that true?

Today, this view of nature dominates Western academic culture.

Some contemporary scientists attempt to understand the entire universe and life on earth without reference to God, as if something just somehow happened. Everything we see is supposedly like a machine that no one built and no one operates.

But when we think of the natural world as independent of a higher intelligence, a significant problem arises. For the scientist to study nature, nature must have an underlying rational order that the scientist can grasp.

If the natural world was random and lacked order, scientific study would be impossible. Imagine a topsy-turvy world where water freezes at 32 degrees one day and 50 degrees the next. In that world, a scientist would be out of a job.

Einstein once remarked that the most incomprehensible thing about the world is that it is comprehensible. In fact, he saw the world's comprehensibility as a miracle (his word) that the increase of scientific knowledge constantly reinforced. Nature is not the confusing world of *Alice in Wonderland*, but an orderly place that our minds seem ideally suited to understand. This is one of the great questions confronting the scientist: Why is the world ordered, and what is the origin of that order?

Why the world is law-governed is ultimately a question not for science but for philosophy. Science presupposes that the world is law-governed. Science cannot progress without basic philosophical commitments about the nature of the world and of humanity. Science depends on a consistent order in nature. Yet according to Darwinism, our minds were not designed to understand the world but have evolved through a blind, material process to aid survival.

But here is a question the naturalist must face: If the world evolved without a guiding intelligence, why should we be able to understand it at all? If the human mind evolved for the sake of survival (rather than for the sake of knowing truth, which is a very different thing), why should it be trusted?

Charles Darwin understood this problem. "The horrid doubt always arises whether the conviction of man's mind, which has developed from the mind of the lower animals, are of any value or at all trustworthy. Would anyone trust the conviction of a monkey's mind, if there are any convictions in such a mind?"[1] To do science, you have to believe that the world is dependable and logical.

The rational order of the world, as we have seen, poses a serious problem for naturalists. Templeton Prize–winning physicist Paul Davies agrees:

> Science is based on the assumption that the universe is thoroughly rational and logical at every level. Atheists claim that the laws [of nature] exist reasonlessly and that universe is ultimately absurd. As a scientist, I find this hard to accept. There must be an unchanging rational ground in which the logical, orderly nature of the universe is rooted.[2]

BRAINS AS SURVIVAL MACHINES

"Our highly developed brains, after all, were not evolved under the pressure of discovering scientific truths but only to enable us to be clever enough to survive and leave descendants."[3]

FRANCIS CRICK, CODISCOVERER OF THE DOUBLE HELIX

"Our brains were shaped for fitness, not for truth. Sometimes the truth is adaptive, but sometimes it is not."[4]

HARVARD COGNITIVE SCIENTIST STEVE PINKER

Natural Versus Spiritual

In the West, there are two primary options for explaining the order in the world: (1) a divine intelligence created the world to be ordered (creation), or (2) nature operates only by material forces and has the power to order itself (naturalism). Two of the most fundamental questions we can ask are these: Why is the world ordered? And where did the order come from?

The media often portray a self-ordered world as scientific and a divinely ordered world as religious. But actually both ways of seeing the world are religious. Naturalism (believing nature is all there is) is as much a religious commitment as theism (believing God is the prime reality). The Supreme Court agrees, having ruled that a belief system is religious if it is "a sincere and meaningful belief which occupies in the life of its possessor a place parallel to that filled by traditional belief in God."[5]

The justices were right. Religion is not necessarily a set of beliefs about God. Some traditional religions, such as Buddhism, don't believe in God. Secular humanists, who also don't believe in God, often organize themselves in church-like and parachurch-like groups. Julian Huxley, first director-general of UNESCO, even wanted to start a religion of evolution in the 1950s.

The Court referred to the work of theologian Paul Tillich, who held that all people—whether theist, atheist, or otherwise—have an ultimate commitment of one sort or another. This ultimate commitment acts as a unifying principle in their lives (even if they don't realize it). It is this ultimate commitment that is religious.

The order we find in the world may come from a creator God, or it may come from the self-ordering powers of nature. Both views are religious commitments in the Supreme Court's sense. The key question, therefore, is this: Which religious commitment best describes the world we find ourselves in?

Modern science confronts us with new information, but the question itself is not a new one. The apostle Paul distinguishes between people who recognize God's creative action in the world and those who are blind to it. He says the first type of person is spiritual, and the other type is natural (1 Corinthians 2:14-15).

A Christian worldview encourages us to recognize God's action in the world. A naturalistic worldview, by contrast, encourages us to see the world merely as a self-contained system. But naturalism is a depressing perspective. It offers no hope beyond the immediate future (after you die, you're worm food). We would also argue that it is demonstrably untrue.

When we split the world from God, we prevent people from personally knowing Him. We prevent them from realizing that the unhappiness they experience comes not from blind, purposeless nature but from the consequences of human sin, which is a choice. Neither nature nor nurture ultimately determines us. We can be different, but we must first want to be different, and we need God's help for that.

Nature and Idolatry

If God does not exist, then sin and guilt are illusions. Rather than showing us to be accountable to a personal creator, naturalism leaves one accountable merely to the laws of nature. While there are rewards and punishments with God, there are only consequences with nature.

In fact, if naturalism is true, we cannot even speak of sin because sin implies that an offense has been committed against a person—ultimately, the person of God. But naturalism tells us that God does not exist and that other humans are merely cogs in nature's wheel. To talk about sinning against nature makes no sense. If naturalism is true, we can live whichever way we choose. Our choices may have consequences, but whatever we can get away with is fair game. Many people view such a move as liberating. The biblical writers see it as idolatry.

WHY EMBRACE A MEANINGLESS WORLD?

"For myself, as, no doubt, for most of my contemporaries, the philosophy of meaninglessness was essentially an instrument of liberation. The liberation we desired was simultaneously liberation from a certain political and economic system and liberation from a certain system of morality. We objected to the morality because it interfered with our sexual freedom; we objected to the political and economic system because it was unjust.

The supporters of these systems claimed that in some way they embodied the meaning (a Christian meaning, they insisted) of the world. There was one admirably simple method of confuting these people and at the same time justifying ourselves in our political and erotical revolt: we could deny that the world had any meaning whatsoever."[6]

ALDOUS HUXLEY

As a child in Sunday school, I (Sean) found the idolatry of the Israelites to be quite silly. I wondered what could possibly motivate people to fashion an idol from a piece of wood, rock, or precious metal and then worship it. Couldn't they see that they had made it themselves? What were they thinking?

But I simply misunderstood what idolatry is. Idolatry does not simply mean thinking some object is special, such as a golden calf or a portrait of a now-dead grandparent who loved us very much. Rather, it means elevating a part of creation above the creator. The Israelites, in worshipping the golden calf, elevated the natural forces represented by the calf above the true God, who had created those natural forces.

Idolatry is, as Rob Lacey puts it, living "for the product instead of the producer."[7] It's having the most basic priorities of life out of whack. Perhaps we don't physically bow before computers, plasma TVs, or iPods—that would be silly. But sometimes we live for these things and many others, elevating them way beyond where they should be. We ask them to fill a role in our lives that only God can and should fill.

CAREER IDOLATRY

"The most hyped of the new shows is 'The Rebel Billionaire,' in which egomaniacal billionaire Richard Branson, owner of Virgin Airlines, torments—yes, you guessed it—money-grubbing weasels willing to debase themselves for a chance to work for him.

Naturalism is idolatry because it raises the creation, conceived as impersonal nature, above the creator. It does this in one of two ways. Either it erases the creator altogether (saying that there is no God) or it puts the creator out of a job (saying that God makes no difference). The naturalist doesn't bow before and pray to his backyard garden, but he raises nature to an improper role, one that only God should fill.

The temptation to worship the created world rather than the creator is ever present. When we forget that God is the creator, sustainer, providential guide, and redeemer of this world, we readily succumb to idolatry.

Rather than thank God, naturalistic scientists will therefore thank nature. The late Harvard evolutionist Stephen Jay Gould is a case in point. Note his remark about the destruction of the dinosaurs:

> Since dinosaurs were not moving toward markedly larger brains, and since such a prospect may lie outside the capabilities of reptilian design...we must assume that consciousness would not have evolved on our planet if a cosmic catastrophe had not claimed the dinosaurs as victims. *In an entirely literal sense, we owe our existence, as large and reasoning animals, to our lucky stars.*[9]

In fact, we have no idea how our emergence would have been affected if some dinosaurs had survived the catastrophe. Perhaps the most popular exhibits at zoos would be Jurassic parks, but what about more serious outcomes? According to Gould, we "must assume" that consciousness happened by accident and that it would not have happened if the dinosaurs had not gone extinct.

And what does he offer as evidence? Only that dinosaurs were not moving toward larger brains. But then neither were most creatures who survived. Human consciousness is unique, just as the human brain is unique. Gould does not offer a credible explanation for why we owe our existence to our lucky stars. But many people accept his premise without thinking carefully about the poor quality of the evidence that supports it.

Scripture uses many words and images to portray idolatry, but the most fitting is *foolishness*. To engage in idolatry is utter foolishness, but the reality is that we *all* do it or have done it. Naturalists are not the only ones who commit idolatry. At some point, all of us are guilty of raising creation—or some aspect of creation—above the creator. Idolatry is utter foolishness because it elevates what is second-best over what is best. An idolater is like a person who, given a chance to drive a Ferrari, preferred to stay home and play with a matchbox version of it.

The creation is awe-inspiring, so we can understand why we fall in love with it. Watching *Planet Earth* inspires awe. But as Maximus the Confessor reminds us in his *Four Centuries on Love*, if the creation is so marvelous, how much more marvelous is the one who created it! The creation is good and even very good. But it is not best. God is best. In fact, God is so much better than what is second-best that to place Him at the same level as anything else is utter foolishness.

Naturalism and Western Culture

Naturalism is everywhere in Western culture. We see it whenever the miracles of Jesus are explained as crowd psychology, often by clergy or professors of religion. We see it whenever a PBS nature program credits nature rather than God for some remarkable wonder like the march of the penguins. We see it when psychologists claim that we lie or cheat because our supposed cave ancestors transmitted lying or cheating genes to us—ignoring that we are fallen beings created in the image of God. And we see it in popular culture whenever created things are elevated above the creator.

Despite the dominance of naturalism in Western culture, Christians are right to remain unconvinced. God created nature as well as any laws by which nature operates. God not only created the world but also upholds the world moment by moment. Colossians 1:15-17 makes this clear in its hymn of praise to Jesus Christ, the second person of the Trinity:

> He is the image of the invisible God, the firstborn of all creation. For by Him all things were created, both in the heavens and on earth, visible and invisible, whether thrones or dominions or rulers or authorities—all things have been created through Him and for Him. He is before all things, and in Him all things hold together.

All the non-Christians I (Sean) have met seemed to tolerate my personal belief in a creator God as long as it was just a personal opinion, backed by no evidence. As long as believers maintain that God's existence is merely a matter of personal belief or preference, we tend to be left alone.

Though not always. I (Bill) have to deal with militant atheists such as Richard Dawkins (author of *The God Delusion*), who think that science has disproved God and that belief in God is a communicable disease that needs to be eradicated. Dawkins, at a Stanford forum on science education, remarked that his goal is "to kill religion."[10]

In any case, controversy arises as soon as Christians assert that evidence supports God's interaction with the world. I (Sean) once sat next to a geologist on a plane, and we had a very pleasant conversation, even when the topic turned to religion. But when I told her I was unconvinced by Darwinian evolution and that I believed the existence of a designer was detectable in nature, you would have thought I said the word *bomb* on the plane!

Personal belief in God is one thing, but the stakes change completely if you say that His existence is supported by actual evidence. No wonder the debate over God's existence is heating up: More and more people have begun to understand and be persuaded by the evidence for God from nature.

The Scientific Question

This book examines the evidence that nature reveals for a designer. This is a scientific question, not merely a question of personal faith or religious experience. Yet to answer this question fairly, our science must not be restricted by naturalism. If we determine in advance that science can only investigate natural causes, we rule out the possibility of a designer before the investigation has even begun.

Consider detectives investigating a suspicious death. The death could be due to an accident or a heart attack. But it could also be due to foul play. Respectable detectives must be open to both natural causes and intelligent ones, and they must be able to distinguish between the two well enough to satisfy the strict standards of a courtroom. Otherwise, many killers would get off scot-free.

Intelligent causes can do things that natural causes cannot. And that is how we detect them. For instance, natural causes can account for the random arrangement of Scrabble pieces on a board. But if the letters spelled out "Let's all meet up at the Snack Shack" we would know that an intelligence arranged them. Just as this meaningful sentence points beyond itself to an intelligent agent, so too nature—from the smallest cell to the structure of the universe—points to intelligent activity.

Intelligent Design to the Rescue

Were you to walk across an open field and stumble upon an ordinary rock, you would probably not conclude it was the result of any particular design. The forces of nature—including wind, rain, and the movement of earth's plates—explain its composition, location, and appearance. But if you found a watch in that same field, the watch's adaptation of means to an end (that is, its ability to tell time) would convince you that it was not simply the result of natural forces but of design. This, of course, is the famous watchmaker argument, made popular by William Paley in the nineteenth century.[11]

Though intuitively appealing, design arguments such as Paley's fell into disrepute until recently. Darwin supposedly provided the nail in the coffin for design arguments. Scientist Francis Ayala put it this way: "It was Darwin's greatest accomplishment to show that the complex organization and functionality of living beings can be explained as the result of a natural process—natural selection—without any need to resort to a Creator or other external agent."[12]

Despite such confident proclamations, a very different story is emerging from the study of nature. Indeed, evidence for design is exploding.[13] Today, design can be rigorously formulated as a scientific theory. What has hindered recognition of design ever since Darwin is the absence of precise methods for identifying design in nature. For design to be a fruitful scientific theory, scientists need a reliable method for recognizing intelligence.

Intelligent design has emerged as a new program for scientific research. In biology, intelligent design is a theory of biological origins and development. Its basic claim is that intelligent causes best explain the complex, information-rich structures of biology and that these causes are detectable by the methods of science. In other words, intelligent causation is empirically detectable.

Many particular sciences have already developed such methods for recognizing design, including forensic science, cryptography, archaeology, and the search for extraterrestrial intelligence (as seen in the movie *Contact*). Intelligent design does not have to prove that it is a science—it already is a science.

Evolution, Creation, and Intelligent Design

Evolution

One of the most common questions I (Bill) get when speaking on intelligent design is, "How does ID fit into the creation-evolution debate?" To answer this question fairly, it is important to be clear on what we mean by *evolution, creation,* and *intelligent design.*

Evolution can mean many different things, which is why a precise definition is critical. Some meanings are uncontroversial, such as that things change over time or that organisms adapt to their changing environments. Common examples include bacteria developing resistance to antibiotics or finch beaks varying in size over weather cycles. This is small-scale evolution, known as *microevolution,* and no one disputes it.

As helpful as the idea of microevolution is to biology, it is irrelevant to the larger claims of Darwinism. In microevolution no new species crop up—bacteria remain bacteria and finches remain finches.

Controversy and confusion arise, however, when Darwinists claim that microevolution leads inevitably to *macroevolution*—radical, dramatic change that produces completely new species. Darwinists assert, without evidence, that organisms have unlimited ability to change. Macroevolution is a central feature of Darwinism. Darwinism makes two big claims:

1. All organisms (life forms) are related back through time to a common ancestor. This is typically called *common descent* or *universal common ancestry.*

2. The process that brought all organisms into existence from a common ancestor is natural selection acting on random variations. This process operates by chance and necessity, apart from any evident intention or direct design.

Darwin argued that nature would select the fittest organisms—the stronger, quicker, healthier ones—to survive and produce offspring. That is called natural selection, and it is not a controversial idea. We see it in nature every day. The controversial part is the claim that this process alone can lead to the emergence of new species.

According to contemporary neo-Darwinism, one organism

becomes more fit than another through random mutation of genes—or, in laymen's terms, sheer luck. Though most mutations are harmful and some are neutral, Darwinists bank on the occasional positive mutation to prop their theory. Given enough positive mutations and enough time for natural selection to act on them, evolution could account for all the complexity and diversity in the biological world, without need for intelligent guidance. In fact, intelligence would then be the result of evolution rather than something that guides it.

That is the way the word *evolution* is used in science classes today. It means Darwinian macroevolution, not microevolution. Nevertheless, many people confuse the evidence for microevolution with evidence for macroevolution. After a *Newsweek* article on evolution, one respondent wrote in to the editor in defense of Darwinism: "They say there's no evidence for evolution. Yet there it is within my own lifetime. My older sister was one of the patients saved by the new wonder drug penicillin, which probably couldn't save her now because microbes have evolved to the point that penicillin can't kill them anymore. That's fact, not theory—evidence that life forms can change over time."[14]

Can you spot the confusion? She offers evidence for microevolution, but her example is irrelevant to the grand claims of Darwinism. If, in order to beat the antibiotic, the bacteria had evolved into jellyfish, *that* would be evidence for Darwin's theory. But no such transition has ever been observed.

So how *does* ID fit into the evolution-creation debate? The intelligent design community is a broad tent. We have only begun to glimpse how design gets implemented and expressed in the fabric of nature. Some argue that God continually intervenes in nature to create new species. Others accept common descent, arguing that God front-loaded the universe with information for it to evolve.

Biochemist Michael Behe, author of *The Edge of Evolution,* for instance, accepts common descent but argues that it requires intelligent guidance. Behe believes that apes and humans share a common ancestor, but he rejects Darwin's claim that random variation and natural selection alone explain how that happened. Thus, he accepts the first tenet of Darwinism above but rejects the second.

Many other ID theorists, on the other hand, reject common descent. Developmental biologist Jonathan Wells, coauthor of *The Design of Life*, for instance, sees fossil and molecular data as so full of gaps as to overthrow the gradual pattern of organismal change predicted by Darwin's theory.

ID theorists may disagree over common descent, but they agree that organisms show clear, scientific evidence of design. Darwin's theory, in their view, is false. The primary question for intelligent design is not *how* organisms came to be (though they regard that as an important question also). Rather, it is whether organisms demonstrate clear, observable marks of being intelligently caused.

Theistic Evolution

Unlike intelligent design, which clashes with Darwinism, theistic evolution holds that God used Darwinian evolution to produce the diversity and complexity of life forms on earth. Theistic evolutionists consider belief in God consistent with Darwinian evolution.

According to theistic evolution, the biological world shows no scientific evidence for the existence of a designer. The biological world may appear designed, but that appearance of design is either a religious intuition or an artifact of evolution (which produces things that appear to be designed but really are not). Theistic evolution is scientifically indistinguishable from atheistic evolution, claiming that the universe provides no scientific evidence for intelligent causes.

One might ask, if undirected material causes are so effective at "designing" the world, why invoke God at all? Theistic evolution seems to put God out of a job or make Him a master of stealth who never shows His hand.

Theistic evolution sidesteps the key question: Does hard scientific evidence of design exist in nature? If so, can we discover evidence of God's existence? The answer is obvious: Put nature to the test and see where the evidence points. This is precisely what intelligent design does—it has us do the scientific legwork to determine whether a designer actually is responsible for the physical world.

Creationism

Creationism holds that the universe was created by a supreme being.[15] Creationists come in two stripes: *young-earth creationists* and *old-earth creationists*. Young-earth creationism is based on a particular interpretation of the book of Genesis in the Bible. According to young-earth creationists, God created the world in six 24-hour days, the universe is roughly 10,000 years old, and the fossils that scientists dig up were largely created by Noah's global flood.

Old-earth creationists, on the other hand, allow more latitude in their interpretation of Genesis. They accept standard scientific dating, which places the earth at roughly 4.5 billion years old and the universe at 13.7 billion years old. Moreover, they accept microevolution as God's method of adapting existing species to their changing environments, but they reject macroevolution.

Intelligent design, though often confused with creationism, is in fact quite different from it. Rather than begin with a particular interpretation of Genesis (as young-earth and old-earth creationists typically do), ID begins by investigating the natural world. Given what the natural world tells us about itself, its proponents argue that an intelligent agent best explains certain patterns in nature. Intelligent design provides a platform for Christians of various stripes—including young earth creationists, old-earth creationists, and gap-theorists—to find common ground in making the case for design in nature.

The great difference with creationism, then, is that ID theory relies *not* on prior theological assumptions for recognizing intelligent activity, but on reliable methods developed within the scientific community.[16] Even Judge Jones in the *Kitzmiller v. Dover* trial recognized that ID proponents do not base their theory on the book of Genesis, a young earth, or a catastrophic Noachian flood.

Who Is the Designer?

Intelligent design does not identify the designer. Why not? The question of the identity of the designer goes beyond the scientific evidence for design into philosophy and religion. Most advocates of ID are Christians, but many Jews, Buddhists, Muslims, Hindus, and agnostics see evidence for design in nature. The evidence of science can identify a designer consistent with the God of the Bible (for example, one that is powerful, creative, skilled, and benevolent), but science alone cannot prove that this designer is the God of Christianity or any other religious faith.

This is why ID research can be an effective tool in apologetics. Rather than beginning with religious presuppositions, design theorists appeal to publicly available evidence. That is, they reason from what we can see in nature. They do not begin by asking people to accept that the Bible is true. We do not need to have any opinion about the Bible to see that the universe bears the marks of design.

This is the same tactic I (Sean) use to teach my students how to defend the lives of unborn children threatened by abortion. Rather than assuming the Bible is true, it is much more fruitful to reason *from* science, philosophy, and common sense *to* a biblical view of the unborn. For those willing to honestly consider the evidence, a compelling scientific case can be made that certain features of the world are best explained by an intelligent agent. Are you open to the evidence?

THREE

THE SURPRISING TRUTH

THE EVIDENCE FOR DARWINIAN EVOLUTION IS WEAK. Does that surprise you? Do you have trouble believing it? You may have studied evolution in biology class, viewed fossils at a natural history museum, or watched a TV documentary that exalts Darwin for unlocking life's deepest mysteries. Invariably these sources tell us that the case for Darwinian evolution is overwhelming. In fact, it is underwhelming.

Yes, you do hear a different story from Darwinists. Consider some recent statements:

- "No educated person any longer questions the validity of the so-called theory of evolution, which we now know to be a simple fact."[1]
- "Every bit of information we have gathered about nature is consonant with the theory of evolution, and there is not one whit of evidence contradicting it. Neo-Darwinism, like the theory of chemical bonds, has graduated from theory to fact."[2]
- "Darwin's venerable theory is widely regarded as one of the best supported ideas in science, the only explanation for the diversity of life on Earth, grounded in decades of study and objective evidence."[3]

- "Evolution is fact, *fact*, FACT!"[4]
- "Scientists agree that the evolutionary origin of animals and plants is a scientific conclusion beyond reasonable doubt."[5]

Darwinian evolution is the predominant view held by most scientists today. Even so, truth is not determined by majority vote. The majority of scientists have been wrong many times in the past—as when they initially rejected plate tectonics because they thought continents were immovable—and they will most certainly be wrong again in the future.

Even though many scientists are convinced that evolution is true beyond a reasonable doubt, a growing number of reputable scientists (with Ph.D.s from top secular universities) question Darwin's theory on scientific grounds. Keep in mind that these scientists are not all Christians. Many are Jews, Muslims, or Buddhists, and some are even agnostics!

WHY ID THEORISTS ARE UNIMPRESSED WITH DARWINIAN EVOLUTION

"The magnificent Natural History Museum in London devotes an entire wing to demonstrating the fact of evolution. They show how pink daisies can evolve into blue daisies, how gray moths change into black moths, how over a mere few thousand years, a wide variety of cichlid fish species evolved in Lake Victoria. It is all impressive.

"Impressive, until you walk out and reflect upon that which they were able to document. Daisies remained daisies, moths remained moths, and cichlid fish remained cichlid fish. These changes are referred to as microevolution. In this exhibit, the museum's staff did not demonstrate a single unequivocal case in which life underwent a major gradual morphological change."[6]

JEWISH PHYSICIST GERALD SCHROEDER

Darwinists often say that their theory of evolution is as well established as the prize theories of physics and chemistry. In their view, the evidence for evolution is just as strong as the evidence for Einstein's theory of general relativity. Yet how many physicists claim that general relativity is as well established as Darwinian evolution? The answer is zero.

Bias prevents many Darwinists from following the evidence where it leads. Because of their commitment to naturalism, they consider the case closed before examining both sides. In his history of the intelligent design movement, Thomas Woodward describes the persistent refusal of Darwinists to consider the weaknesses of their theory as "a moral tale of self-deluded blindness, long over-looked, but finally—at great sacrifice—brought to light."[7]

As scientists have started to question Darwinism, many have come to see that scientific evidence—particularly from biology—points compellingly toward a creative intelligence behind life. In publicizing their doubts about Darwin, they have often faced personal and professional persecution. Yet increasing numbers of scientists are willing to take the heat.

Even though Darwinism exerts enormous influence in universities, the media, and Hollywood, the public remains unconvinced. Studies typically show that between 40 and 45 percent of the public holds to a recent-creation view, and another 40 to 45 percent holds that God somehow used evolution as His means to create. Only around 10 percent hold to strict Darwinism.

Darwinists would like to believe that people are skeptical of Darwin's theory because they've been religiously indoctrinated and haven't been properly educated. But this is a curious claim to make given that, for the past 40 years, public schools have exclusively taught Darwinism. Rather than a problem of education, the problem is one of evidence: Darwinism just doesn't have the goods. Despite confident assertions, like those above, the actual evidence in favor of Darwin's grand theory of evolution—as we'll now see—is surprisingly thin.

A guy doesn't take phone calls when he is parachuting into a forest fire. But Washington State biology teacher (and summertime smoke jumper) Roger DeHart happened to be pulling weeds, awaiting a fire call in the summer of 1997, when he was paged to line 1. It was his superintendent.

And the news was amazing. The American Civil Liberties Union (ACLU) was threatening the school board with a lawsuit over the way DeHart taught evolution. "I have always taught evolution. That has never been a question for me," he recalls.

Throughout the 1990s, Roger DeHart had taught high school biology and environmental chemistry at Burlington-Edison High School near Seattle. He was, by all accounts, a popular teacher. Because he was interested in the new theory of intelligent design, he began bringing materials about it to the classroom. Although he is a Christian, he did not talk about God or religion; in fact, he tried to ensure that students could not tell what his position was. He insisted that they argue the case for both sides, and he encouraged them to think.

However, in 1997, one of his students and the student's parents complained to the ACLU that he was teaching about the intelligent design controversy and that this amounted to teaching religion. Hence the threat of a lawsuit. The superintendent investigated and found no impropriety.

Angry letters from the ACLU and the Darwin lobby poured into the school board. Then, in 1998, the ACLU went to the media. To his amazement, DeHart became a cover story in the *Los Angeles Times* and the subject of an attack ad signed by 350 people in his home town. He was subjected to shoddy journalism and a gag order from his principal. And all for raising the topic of intelligent design.

Students tried to defend him, to no avail.

Faced with the threat of a costly lawsuit from ACLU, the school board told DeHart to teach nothing but the text, which provided a standard overview of Darwinism. This overview included material that appears to support Darwinism but is in reality questioned or discredited in the science literature. DeHart was forbidden to provide articles from *Nature* or *The American Biology Teacher* that corrected the errors in the textbook. In his own words, DeHart "was told not to teach anything but the text even if it is wrong."

When DeHart moved to a new school district, the controversy followed him, including four front-page stories in the local paper. His new administration continued to be besieged by media and by angry letters from the Darwin lobby. Even before he took a new job, he was threatened with reassignment. He finally gave up on public education and now teaches at a private school.[8]

Doubts About Darwinism

In *On the Origin of Species,* Darwin made a statement often ignored today. He said, "A fair result can be obtained only by fully stating and balancing the facts and arguments on both sides of each question."[9] Darwin himself believed in considering the evidence on both sides of his theory. But you won't read in today's textbooks that there are problems with Darwinian evolution. When that evidence is weighed, the case for Darwinism is unconvincing.[10] Let's now turn to some of that evidence.

Do Humans Have a Tailbone?

In a recent discussion about evolution, a medical student asked me (Sean), "What about the human tailbone? Isn't it a leftover from our ancestors who had tails?" Such "leftovers" are known as vestigial structures. They are supposed to have performed a useful function at some point in the past, but through some evolutionary changes, they lost their usefulness.

According to Darwinists, the survival of a vestigial structure indicates the existence of a common ancestor for whom the structure formerly served a useful function. Thus science writer Michael Shermer says, "Vestigial structures stand as evidence of the mistakes, the misstarts, and, especially, the leftover traces of evolutionary history."[11]

Yet to count as evidence for evolution, vestigial structures must truly be functionless. A century ago, medical scientists commonly asserted that many structures in the human body were vestigial. Fifty years ago, doctors routinely removed tonsils, adenoids, and appendixes from children. Today, these structures are regarded as functioning parts of the immune system, and their removal is discouraged unless they are infected. Yes, we can live without them, but that is not because they are useless. It is because our immune systems contain numerous backup systems. That is, we are better protected when many organs in a system overlap in their functions. Otherwise, a routine failure might easily be fatal.

So is the coccyx (the human tailbone) a vestige reminiscent of an evolutionary past when our ancestors had tails? Medical textbooks say no. The coccyx plays a crucial role in connecting muscles to the pelvis. Similarly, the human appendix—formerly thought to be vestigial—is now known to play an important role in the immune system. Many functions have been found for biological structures once thought functionless.

Evolutionists counter that some structures in nature truly are vestigial. For instance, certain cave-dwelling salamanders have nubs but no actual eyes. This is a good case of "use it or lose it." At some point in the past, these cave-dwelling creatures lost their eyes. So is this evidence for Darwin's grand theory of evolution?

Eyeless salamanders are certainly consistent with natural selection. If the salamanders don't need eyes, they will not die if they lose them. But Darwin wasn't simply trying to tell us that natural selection occurs; he argued that it has creative power. And the blind cave salamanders represent the exact opposite of creative power. They didn't gain eyes, they lost them.

Ironically, they are evidence for *devolution*, the exact opposite of Darwinian evolution! In devolution, an organism begins with a function and then loses it. Rather than building a new structure from the ground up—as evolution requires—this is an example of a structure breaking down and ceasing to function anymore. But the crucial question for evolution is this: How did the original structure emerge in the first place?

Contrary to what Darwinists have argued, vestigial structures are quite consistent with intelligent design. From the perspective of ID, species were originally designed, but through accident or disuse those structures simply lost their function, as in the case of the salamander eyes.

Vestigial structures may make sense from an evolutionary standpoint, but they also make sense from the perspective of design. Therefore, since both theories can explain the evidence, the existence of vestigial structures cannot count as evidence for or against either theory.

Did the Designer Mess Up?

After graduating from high school, many of my (Sean's) students go to various campuses of the University of California. Many UC students are required to take an introductory class on world history, which begins with the evolution of man. Naturalism pervades these classes, and naturalistic evolution is treated as an established fact.

A couple of years ago, one of the professors decided to hold a forum to allow skeptical students to voice their doubts about Darwinism and to make a case for intelligent design. Two of my former students, now at UC, showed up.

After discussing the merits of intelligent design at some length, the professor raised one of the most common objections—imperfect design. He said that the human eye is evidence against design because it is flawed. One of my former student shot back, "Why is it necessary for design to imply perfection? We design flawed things all the time. Have you ever used Microsoft Word?"

Her point was simple yet profound: Design does not have to be perfect; it just has to be good enough. Even though each edition of

Microsoft Word has some imperfections, it was obviously designed; it did not evolve without guidance from programmers. The mere fact that we think we can imagine a better design doesn't mean the structure we observe lacks design.

What is true for Microsoft Word is equally true in biology. Living systems bear clear marks of design, even if such design is or appears to be imperfect. In reality, there is no such thing as perfect design.

Real designers strive for the best overall compromise among constraints in order to achieve a function. All design involves concessions, give-and-take. For example, a larger computer screen may be easier to work with than a smaller one, but designers must also consider cost, weight, size, and transportability. Given competing factors, designers choose the best overall compromise—and this is what we see in nature too.

For instance, all life forms are part of an ecology that recycles its life forms. All life forms must die. Few life forms live on raw chemical elements or compounds. Most survive by eating living or dead life forms.

Suppose we object to the fact that rabbits get caught and eaten by foxes. If rabbits had perfect defenses, foxes would starve. Then rabbits, having eaten up the vegetation, would starve too. So that uncatchable rabbit would be far more of a problem than a solution for the future of life on earth.

Now let's look again at the eye. What, exactly, is supposed to be wrong with the healthy human eye? The eye is the most commonly cited example of imperfect design. Those critical of its design argue that it is built upside down and backward. But there are good reasons for the eye to be constructed as it is (see the sidebar). Moreover, no one has demonstrated how the eye's function might be improved without diminishing its visual speed, sensitivity, and resolution.

The photoreceptors in the human eye are oriented away from incoming light and placed behind nerves through which light must pass before reaching the photoreceptors. Why?

A visual system needs three things: speed, sensitivity, and resolution. The inverse wiring does not affect speed. Nor does it affect resolution, except for a tiny blind spot in each eye. You don't usually notice it because your brain's visual harmonization system easily compensates for the blind spot. You need to do special exercises to discover it.

What about sensitivity? Sensitivity *requires* an inverted retina. Retinal cells require the most oxygen of any cells in the human body, so they need lots of blood. But blood cells absorb light. In fact, if blood cells invade the retinal cells, irreversible blindness may result.

By facing away from the light, retinal cells can be nourished by blood vessels that do not block the light. They can still be so sensitive that they respond to a single photon, the smallest unit of light.

Octopuses and squid are said to have correctly wired retinas that face outward. But they are exothermic (cold-blooded). They do not have the same oxygen and blood needs as mammals, so their eye wiring is irrelevant.[12]

But what if the eye's functions could be improved so that, for instance, no one ever needed eyeglasses? That would merely demonstrate its lack of perfection, not its lack of design. If Darwinism were true, we might expect to see imperfections in nature, but so too with design. Imperfections alone do nothing to confirm Darwin's theory or to disconfirm design. In any case, as the great Plato taught us, perfection is not to be found in this material world.

Do Chimpanzees and Humans Share Common DNA?

This morning in the news I (Sean) read a story about the human genetic code. According to the authors, humans may exhibit greater genetic differences from each other than previously thought (although the degree of similarity is still marked). As soon as I read the first line of the story I knew there would be a reference to one of the most common evidences offered for Darwinism—the genetic similarity between humans and apes. I read a little further and, sure enough, there it was.

In recent years, genome mapping has enabled detailed comparisons between the DNA of humans and chimpanzees. Many have claimed that humans and chimpanzees share 98 percent of their DNA. This is often taken as decisive evidence of ape-to-human evolution. Besides the genetic similarity, the body structure, including muscles, bones, and organs, is remarkably similar. Doesn't this prove common descent? Interestingly, even if the DNA evidence supported common descent, we can't show that Darwin's mechanism is the cause. The process still may have required design.

In reality, the genetic differences between humans and chimpanzees are probably greater than 2 percent. Recent studies have indicated that the true genetic divergence between humans and apes is actually closer to 5 percent.[13] So the claims that humans and chimpanzees share 98 percent DNA similarity may be overblown.

Because of the complex ways that cells use genetic information, seemingly small genetic change can radically alter biological function. Even if we grant only a 2 percent difference between humans and chimpanzees, consider some of the physical differences between apes and humans:

1. The feet of chimpanzees can grasp anything their hands can. But this is not true for humans.

2. Humans have a nose and chin that stick out, but apes do not.

3. Human females are the only primates that experience menopause.

4. Humans have a fatty inner skin like whales and hippos, but apes do not.

5. Humans sweat, but apes do not.

6. Humans are the only primates who cry.[14]

As interesting as genetic similarities between chimpanzees and humans are, they are not evidence for Darwinism. Design is also able to explain them. Designers often make different products using similar parts, materials, and arrangements. When designers find a pattern or design that works, they often stick with it, even for different products. (For instance, consider the different Apple products.)

Why couldn't the designer of nature use some similar DNA and body structure for different organisms as well? Genetic similarity between chimps and humans does make sense from an evolutionary standpoint, but it is also consistent with intelligent design. Once again, the evidence does not support Darwinism.

Darwin's Most Convincing Evidence

Darwin knew that the fossil record of his day did not support his claims for common descent. He was convinced that, given enough time, the geological record would prove his theory correct. But because the fossil record was not going to help him much, he believed that the most convincing evidence for his theory could be found in embryology, the study of how organisms develop from the time they are conceived to the time they are born or hatched.

Darwin claimed to find remarkable similarities between how the embryos of different species developed. He considered these similarities as "by far the strongest single class of facts in favor of" his theory.[15] Even today, renowned scientists such as Francisco Ayala consider embryonic development as convincing evidence for evolution.[16]

But Darwin was not an expert in embryology. As a result, he drew his evidence from others. He relied especially on Ernst Haeckel, a German biologist. Haeckel reasoned that the development of embryos in the womb (or egg) mirrors the larger evolutionary process of nature. In other words, an individual embryo will develop in a pattern similar to the evolutionary development of the species.

For instance, because humans are thought to have evolved from fish, a human embryo might develop as a fish before developing obviously human characteristics. Darwin found this pattern so convincing that he said, "It is probable, from what we know of the embryos of mammals, birds, fishes and reptiles, that these animals are the modified descendants of some ancient progenitor."[17]

To make his point, Haeckel made drawings of various embryos such as chickens, frogs, and fish. He wanted to show that the early embryos of different species look very much the same but then become noticeably different as they develop. His drawings had a great influence on popular culture because they were reprinted many times.

Even though Haeckel's drawings still appear in some textbooks today, it has been known for over a century that they were faked. Yes, *faked!* Haeckel cherry-picked his examples, and even then he still had to exaggerate similarities. Rather than representing embryological development accurately, Haeckel skewed his drawings to fit his theory.

The late Stephen Jay Gould, who was no friend to ID theorists, noted that "Haeckel had exaggerated the similarities by idealizations and omissions. He also, in some cases—in a procedure that can only be called fraudulent—simply copied the same figure over and over again."[18] In an interview for *Science,* Michael Richardson put it bluntly: "It looks like it's turning out to be one of the most famous fakes in biology."[19]

The actual embryonic evidence is quite different from what Darwin had hoped: Vertebrate embryos do not look very similar in the early stages and then begin to differ in the later stages. Haeckel and Darwin took the most similar stages and arbitrarily considered them the "first" stages of development. When the actual first stages of embryonic development are considered, their evidence collapses—the embryos start out very different.

Even though scientists know that the earliest stages of embryological development are not the most similar ones, the drawings are still in use in many textbooks today (many others use carefully selected but still misleading photos). When confronted with these facts, many Darwinists admit that the drawings may have been faked but insist that that's okay because they illustrate a "deeper truth" about evolution.

Embryologist Jonathan Wells concludes, "So when the strongest facts in favor of Darwin's theory turn out not to be facts at all, what do Darwinists do? Rather than question the theory, as scientists in other fields might, Darwinists simply declare that theory is true anyway and use it to explain away those pesky embryos."[20]

Can Jurassic Park Save the Day?

Jurassic Park was a watershed movie. When it first came out, people were blown away by the dazzling portrayal of dinosaurs on the big screen. I (Sean) got a chill down my spine the first time I saw the famous *Tyrannosaurus rex* chase scene. But perhaps the main reason for the movie's success was its believability. People imagined that, given advances in our understanding of the genetic basis of life, dinosaur DNA could be inserted into an ostrich egg to form a *Tyrannosaurus rex*. Yet as believable as this movie may seem, it is pure science fiction.

The development of an organism is determined not merely by DNA but also by features of the surrounding egg and cell membrane. Despite what is commonly believed, DNA does not contain all the information necessary for the development of an organism. That, incidentally, is why there is so much confusion over the cloning debate: If you took your DNA and inserted it into a human egg that had its own DNA removed, you would not have an exact (although younger) replica of yourself. How your "clone" looked would depend not only on the DNA but also on the information in the enucleated egg that received your DNA.

If DNA does not solely determine the development of an

organism, is it possible for a new species to emerge through mutations in existing DNA? A recent proposal by Darwinists says yes: "Evo-devo," a shortened name for *evolutionary developmental biology*—looks to genes in early development to determine if the right mutations in them could lead to macroevolutionary change. According to evo-devo, the right mutation early in the development of an organism might lead to major changes later on—perhaps even to the development of a new species.

To illustrate this idea, imagine an arrow aimed right at a target. If left undisturbed, the arrow would fly straight into the bull's eye. Yet the sooner in flight it is disturbed, the greater the distance by which it will miss the target. Similarly, evo-devo proponents argue that the mutation of a few key genes in early development could eventually lead to significant macroevolutionary changes in an entire species. So, what natural selection might not do in general, it might do through certain genes in an early embryo.

Of course, mutations can only assist evolution if they benefit the organism. The problem for evo-devo is that mutations in developmental genes never benefit the organism and are almost always harmful.

Biologists have found that mutations in developmental genes often lead to death or deformity. Evo-devo experts work a lot with fruit flies. Tweaking one developmental gene in a fruit fly can lead to an extra set of wings. Unfortunately, those wings don't have muscles and are therefore worse than useless—they make it harder for the fly to fly.

So is this the mechanism that can account for Darwinian evolution? No. As Jonathan Wells explains, "All of the evidence points to one conclusion: no matter what we do to a fruit fly embryo, there are only three possible outcomes—a normal fruit fly, a defective fruit fly, or a dead fruit fly. Not even a horsefly, much less a horse."[21]

Mutations have sometimes led to minor changes within a species—such as bacteria and insecticide resistance—but there are no known cases where such mutations have produced large-scale changes that benefit an organism, let alone the development of a new species. Mutations may be able to help bacteria survive (microevolution), but they are incapable of producing any kind of new species, much less transform a cow into a whale or a dinosaur into a bird (macroevolution). Such transformation requires intelligent coordination. This is why biologist William Jeffery admits that evo-devo's efforts to understand how developmental genes induce macroevolutionary change is "at a dead end."[22]

HIV Mutations

The final evidence for evolution we want to consider in this chapter is HIV resistance to antiviral drugs. HIV is short for human immunodeficiency virus, which is thought to be the cause of AIDS (acquired immunodeficiency syndrome). Viruses are bits of genetic material enclosed by a protective protein coating. They are incapable of reproducing by themselves (and therefore not alive), but they are capable of reproducing by hijacking the genetic machinery of cells (and thereby usually killing the cells). Darwinist Jerry Coyne makes this claim:

> Biologists have now observed hundreds of cases of natural selection, beginning with the well-known examples of bacterial resistance to antibiotics, insect resistance to DDT and HIV resistance to antiviral drugs...And the strength of selection observed in the wild, when extrapolated over long periods, is more than adequate to explain the diversification of life on Earth.[23]

Is this true? Are mutations in the HIV virus good evidence for macroevolution? In one sense, the above quote *is* true. Antibiotics, DDT, and the HIV virus provide great examples of natural selection in action. But here is the key question: Can the minor changes witnessed in the HIV virus (microevolution) be extrapolated to account for all "the diversification of life on Earth" (macroevolution)? Recent evidence indicates the exact opposite of what Coyne and others claim about HIV.

HIV is a virus. As such, it contains far less genetic information than a cell and therefore mutates extraordinarily quickly. Thus, HIV is a great test case for the limits of natural selection. With millions of people infected worldwide, the HIV virus has undergone myriads of mutations.[24] Thus, HIV could potentially demonstrate whether natural selection acting on random mutations can help positively develop life, as Darwin claimed.

So, what have these mutations wrought? Biochemist Michael Behe, author of *The Edge of Evolution*, says, "*Very little.* Although news stories rightly emphasize the ability of HIV to quickly develop drug resistance, and although massive publicity makes HIV seem to the public to be an evolutionary powerhouse, on a functional biochemical level the virus has been a complete stick-in-the-mud."[25]

The HIV virus has not undergone the breathtaking changes we should expect if natural selection were as powerful as Darwin claimed. HIV functions exactly as it did when first discovered roughly 50 years ago. Although minor changes within HIV have enabled it to resist certain drugs, nothing fundamentally new has emerged. And this is true for malaria, *E. coli,* and all other laboratory organisms studied by scientists for the past century. Claiming that HIV and other bacterial resistance supports macroevolution is a leap of faith unwarranted by the evidence.

Intelligent guidance is the only known cause that can explain the large-scale coordinated changes that Darwin's theory is supposed to explain but doesn't. Natural selection can weed out the unfit, but it is a non-intelligent process incapable of building the integrated systems we see in biology, such as the cell. The ability of organisms to undergo small-scale adaptive changes is itself best explained as a part of the original design of life.

Ready for the Trash Heap?

To appreciate the true state of Darwinism, imagine what would happen to the germ theory of disease if scientists never found any microorganisms or viruses that produced diseases. Obviously, it would be abandoned! Evolutionists have proposed mechanisms to explain small-scale changes in organisms (like HIV developing antiviral resistance). They have *not* shown how such mechanisms can reasonably be extrapolated to explain large-scale changes in organisms, such as bacteria developing the complex molecular machines we will explore in chapter 8. They offer many just-so stories but no detailed, testable models for how it could be done. Without such models, Darwinism is dead in the water.

FOUR

WHAT STORY DO THE ROCKS TELL?

THE PLANE WAS RAPIDLY LOSING ALTITUDE as we prepared to land. I (Sean) had been watching the PBS special *Evolution* on my laptop and was just putting my computer away. The woman next to me looked over, her interest piqued by what I'd been watching.

"So," she began, "what do you think about evolution?" Before I could say anything, she blurted out, "I think it's a fact. After all, museums are filled with fossils that prove evolution is true. Humans and apes had a common ancestor, as well as all other organisms. It's as simple as that."

Was she right? Is it a simple fact that all organisms share a common ancestor? Does the fossil record prove Darwin's theory of evolution? Or does it point to a designer instead?

She was right about one thing: Thousands of fossil remains fill museums today. Museum guides will tell you that they show that all living things trace their lineage back to one, or at most a few, early ancestors. Do they? Let's see.

What Story Do the Rocks Tell?

Scientists who study fossils are known as *paleontologists*. By studying skeletons, footprints, leaves, feathers, eggs, droppings, and many other remains, paleontologists attempt to reconstruct past life forms, many of them extinct. They ask, what story do the rocks tell?

But it's not as simple as just asking a question. Many people underestimate how deeply background assumptions shape the answer given to this question.

A background assumption, for example, of some Hindu people is that cows are the most valuable type of living thing—therefore they are revered and protected. Obviously, this will affect Hindus' diet in ways it does not affect ours. You will not see hamburgers on as many menus in India as you will in America, where that background assumption is rejected. The background assumption of the value of cows, then, shapes the answer to the question, may we have beef for dinner? In the same way, naturalism's background assumptions shape how one interprets the fossil record.

This is difficult for some to accept because we tend to view science as a value-neutral discipline immune to personal bias and subjectivity. Don't scientists set their personal opinions aside and look at the evidence objectively? This is true for many scientific questions that can be verified directly, such as questions about gravity. These questions can often be settled by performing repeatable experiments and drawing reasonable inferences. Yet unlike these scientific questions, which focus on things happening in the present, paleontologists study one-time, non-repeatable historical events far in the past.

Paleontologists are more like detectives working on cold-case files. They look for clues to reconstruct long-past events. Their job is to study the present remains of past events and come up with reasonable explanations that best account for the most facts.

And this is precisely why presuppositions play such an important role in paleontology. If one begins with the assumption that naturalism is true (and that intelligence is ruled out), then regardless of the evidence, the fossil record will be interpreted as the account of blind material forces operating without an overarching purpose. But that assumption may be mistaken, and if it is mistaken, then the interpretations of fossils based on that false assumption are also most likely false. As you will see, intelligent design may provide a more reasonable explanation of the fossil record than Darwin's theory.

Recently, at the Design of Life blog (www.thedesignoflife.net), Canadian journalist Denyse O'Leary interviewed Mark Mathis, longtime TV news reporter and current line producer of the movie *Expelled* (about the persecution that intelligent design scientists face in a culture that assumes that naturalism is true). Mathis talked about *confirmation bias* as he encountered it in both science and media. Here are some excerpts:

DESIGN OF LIFE: You interviewed 150 scientists for your film. I wonder if that's a record. I gather an effort has been made to discredit the film on the grounds that the anti-ID folk were misrepresented, basically that you tricked them into taking part.

MATHIS: It's not surprising. When you're used to a situation where everything that is talked about in books and films fits your dogmatic view—and that's what they've had—and then a film comes along that applies some actual skepticism, naturally they're unhappy.

They had the list of questions we were going to be examining. A controversy takes at least two sides. But they've become very used to only one side.

Apparently they didn't understand that we were really going to do just what we said we were going to do.

One salient point—all of these people are continually speaking to this issue on the Internet, and in books and films. What they told us is consistent with what they say elsewhere.

DESIGN OF LIFE: Had you been interested in ID before you started making the film? Have you learned anything?

MATHIS: Mildly interested. I certainly wasn't carrying on any kind of a crusade for it. What I learned? Oh man, that's a big question. I certainly have learned a tremendous amount about astronomy, biology, physics, probability, logic, reasoning, philosophy, human behavior, confirmation bias—wow!

Darwin's "Gravest Objection" to His Own Theory

According to Darwinism, all organisms trace their lineage back to a common ancestor through an unguided process of slow, gradual transformation that took place over millions and millions of years. Darwin thought that such transformations happened not by sudden leaps, but by "numerous, successive, slight modifications."[1]

Darwin is famous for using the illustration of a tree—"the great Tree of Life." This tree's trunk represents the universal common ancestor for life. Over time, the tree has grown, and new species have appeared on the branches, which, with their modifications, represent that original life form's descendants. As more species evolve, the differences between them have become more pronounced, and major groupings of animals have emerged.

Therefore, according to Darwin's theory, the fossil record should reveal a steady flow of organisms blending smoothly into one another with countless transitional forms (like a color wheel blends different colors almost imperceptibly into one another). Is that what we see?

In fact, the differences between major groups of animals (such as crabs and birds) are so significant that Darwin's theory demands massive numbers of transitional forms. Darwin himself wrote in

The Origin of Species, "The number of intermediate and transitional links, between all living and extinct species, must have been inconceivably great."[2]

Yet when Darwin formulated his theory of evolution, the fossil evidence for an "inconceivably great" number of intermediate and transitional links was utterly lacking. To his credit, Darwin conceded that the absence of transitional forms was a considerable problem for his theory: "Why then is not every geological formation and every stratum full of such intermediate links? Geology assuredly does not reveal any such finely graduated organic chain."[3] Darwin considered this "the most obvious and gravest objection, which can be urged against my theory."[4] He was convinced, though, that paleontologists would eventually find more fossils and vindicate his theory.

Are the Missing Links Still Missing?

Since the publication of *The Origin of Species* roughly 150 years ago, scientists have found a staggering number of fossils unknown to Darwin. In fact, fossils are being discovered today faster than they can be cataloged. But what have *not* been found are the transitional forms Darwin's theory predicts. Rather than filling gaps in the existing record, fossils have tended to add new gaps that refuse to narrow. Although one would not know this from standard biology textbooks, the following statement is true: *The fossil record is even more at odds with Darwin's theory now than it was when he first proposed it.*

The pattern of the fossil record is not the slowly branching tree Darwin imagined, but a collection of distinct clusters separated by gaps. Perhaps this should not surprise us because it is precisely what we see in living organisms today. For instance, there are many varieties of horses, but they are clearly distinct from fish. And there are many varieties of ants, but no one would confuse them with worms.

Admittedly, a few oddballs have shown up that have been difficult to categorize because they have characteristics from widely different organisms. The best-known example is *Archaeopteryx*, a now-extinct bird with reptile-like features. *Archaeopteryx* had feathers, like modern flying birds. But it also had reptile-like features including claws, a toothed jaw, and a bony tail. Since 1861, when it was first discovered, *Archaeopteryx* has been heralded as a missing link between reptiles and birds. But according to most paleontologists today, it is not even a direct ancestor of modern birds. Rather, it is a unique species of bird that is now extinct. In any event, Darwinian theorists now contend that birds are descended from dinosaurs, not reptiles.

A modern example is the duck-billed platypus. This Australian life form has a bill (a highly modified snout) and webbed feet, and—this is its most remarkable trait—it lays eggs like a bird. But it also has mammal-like features such as fur, and it nurses its hatched young on milk. Therefore, despite its birdlike features, the platypus is classified as a mammal. Yet it has never even been entertained as a missing link. Together with the spiny anteaters, the platypus belongs to an unusual, rare order of mammals called *monotremes*.

Most proposed transitional forms are like the *Archaeopteryx* and platypus—they can definitely be classified in one group, even though they share certain features with another group. Moreover, those features all belong fully to one group or another—these organisms do not possess intermediate features.

This is true for ape-to-human evolution as well. Many fossils have been heralded as the missing link between apes and humans, but upon further investigation, they tend to be fully ape or fully human. This has been found to be the case for Java man,[5] Lucy,[6] and Neanderthal man.[7]

British engineer and science journalist Richard Milton sums up the evidence for ape-to-human evolution from the fossil record:

> The position today is that all fossil remains which were previously assigned some intermediate status between apes and humans have later been definitely reassigned

into the categories of either extinct ape or human, and this reassignment has been accepted by all but the most fanatical devotees of this or that fossil...the missing link is still missing.[8]

Striking Features of the Fossil Record

There are three known features of the fossil record that must be explained by any theory of biological origin. Each of these is at odds with Darwinian evolution.

The Biological Big Bang

As you may recall from biology class, scientists typically categorize living organisms into seven broad groupings, from species to kingdom. The most fundamental classification is *kingdom,* which distinguishes living things into plants or animals.

The second basic classification is *phylum* (plural *phyla*), which relates to the basic body plan of the organism. Phyla mark the highest categories in the animal kingdom, each phylum having a unique body plan. There are several dozen phyla, including mollusks, which include squid and octopi; arthropods, which include insects, spiders, and crustaceans; and chordates, which include all backboned animals, such as humans and fish.

At the beginning of the geological era known as the Cambrian period, roughly 530 million years ago by conventional dating, the majority of phyla appeared in a geological blink of an eye and without any trace of a prior evolutionary history. Yet according to Darwinism, phyla should emerge after an inconceivably great number of simpler transitional forms toward the *end* of the evolutionary process. The fossil record, however, reveals no such gradual emergence. Rather, representatives of the major phyla show up in a geological instant (which is why this phenomenon is commonly called the *Cambrian explosion*).

Prior to the Cambrian explosion, the fossil record consists almost exclusively of single-celled organisms, and then—*bam!*—the major animal body plans emerge in a geological moment without any transitional intermediate forms.[9] The Cambrian explosion occurred within an exceedingly narrow window of geologic time, lasting no more than 5 to 10 million years. When compared with the standard history of life on earth (more than 3 billion years), this period of explosion is only a few minutes in a 24-hour day. With few exceptions, new phyla stop appearing after this time period.

Constancy

Once a life form is identified in the fossil record, it persists largely unchanged throughout geological history. In other words, it remains constant. Some exist for a long time and then go extinct. Others still exist today but show no significant change from their first appearance in the fossil record millions of years ago. Rather than revealing organisms at various stages of evolutionary development, the rocks reveal minor changes within various species (microevolution). This is consistent with what breeders have known all along—they can produce interesting and unusual varieties of dogs or roses, but dogs always remain dogs, and roses remain roses.

Gaps

The fossil record appears to follow a rough progression (for instance, fish appear before reptiles, which appear before mammals), but the fossil record fails to support common descent. For example, it does not show a series of gradual fossils connecting fish to amphibians or reptiles to birds. Fossils have features that are fully formed and functional when they first appear in the rocks. The earliest known fish fossils, for example, have all the same characteristics as fish today. And this same pattern is true for all organisms, including reptiles and mammals.

The gaps have become more and more pronounced as fossil discoveries have increased. The lack of fossils with in-between characteristics is a striking feature that cannot be overlooked. This is why the late Harvard paleontologist Stephen Jay Gould noted, "The extreme rarity of transitional forms in the fossil record persists as the trade secret of paleontology. The evolutionary trees that adorn our textbooks have data only at the tips and nodes of their branches; the rest is inference, however reasonable, not the evidence of fossils."[10]

Darwinism Strikes Back

The scarcity of transitional fossils is a vexing problem for Darwinism. Four proposed solutions exist in the scientific literature.

Not Enough Fossils

An imperfect fossil record was Darwin's preferred way of explaining the scarcity of transitional fossils. After all, only a small percentage of the animals that have ever lived became fossils. Most animals that are not consumed by other animals waste away after their deaths and leave no trace. Therefore, say many Darwinists, we should not expect the fossils to be preserved in the first place. Darwin preferred this approach. He put it this way: "The explanation [of the gaps] lies, as I believe, in the extreme imperfection of the geological record."[11]

Yet the key point for judging the state of the fossil record is not the number of fossils, but rather how representative they are of the types of animals that have ever lived. For example, in trying to understand dinosaur evolution, it would be little use to have 800 perfectly preserved tyrannosaurs but no other dinosaur fossil.

In fact, the fossil record appears quite representative of the history of life. We know this by comparing living organisms with the fossil record. For example, among 43 known living orders of land-dwelling vertebrates, 42 have been found as fossils. This is a 98 percent fossilization rate! And among the 329 known living families of terrestrial vertebrates, 261 have been discovered as fossil remains, which is a fossilization rate of nearly 80 percent. If one removes birds (which don't tend to fossilize, in part because their bones are hollow), the fossilization rate is increased to 88 percent.

Not every species gets fossilized, but fossilization percentages at higher levels of classification are quite good. This suggests that in broad strokes the fossil record accurately depicts the history of life on earth. And still the transitional fossils are nowhere to be found.

Look Harder

Perhaps transitional fossils have been preserved, but scientists simply have not found them yet. This may have been a believable explanation in Darwin's day, but today, with big science devoting big budgets to fossil digs, it stretches credibility. We cannot do an exhaustive geological study of the earth, but exhaustive searches have been done of particular areas believed likely to contain transitional fossils. Paleontologists do not stab in the dark; they look for areas where geological history suggests fossils might turn up. And despite the heroic efforts of paleontologists, transitional fossils remain more elusive than ever.

Punctuated Equilibrium

Darwin's theory of slow, gradual evolution finds no support in the fossil record. To explain the scarcity of transitional fossils, some scientists have proposed a modified version of Darwinism known as *punctuated equilibrium*. In this solution, sometimes called *punk-eek,* evolutionary changes take place rapidly in isolated populations over several thousand years. Conventional Darwinism is said to take place slowly over hundreds of millions of years.

So why don't we find the fossils? According to punctuated equilibrium, evolutionary change is so rapid and occurs with such small numbers of transitional animals that they are unlikely to fossilize and thus be represented in the fossil record.

This theory may seem attractive because it agrees with the evidence. But it agrees with the evidence by saying that the evidence that would confirm transitional forms has conveniently disappeared from the fossil record. Simply put, transitional forms, according to punk-eek, have the bad habit of not fossilizing. Punk-eek thereby rationalizes the imperfection of the fossil record.

The biggest challenge for punctuated equilibrium, however, is the same as for conventional Darwinism, which is to explain how an unguided process could produce (whether in long periods or in short bursts) large numbers of new structures and functions. No such explanation is on the horizon.

Supporters of punctuated equilibrium say that gaps in the fossil record support their theory. But might not gaps suggest independent creative acts and therefore argue for design?

Abrupt Emergence

Abrupt emergence is a straightforward interpretation of the fossil record. In other words, we don't find transitional fossils today because they never existed in the first place. There are a number of different sub-theories for this explanation of the fossil record, but they all agree that organisms appeared abruptly and fully formed rather than through a gradual, Darwinian process.

This approach, like punctuated equilibrium, agrees with the evidence. The core problem for most forms of abrupt emergence is the same as for punctuated equilibrium—no known material mechanism can account for such rapid, drastic change. Apart from intelligent design, abrupt emergence seems to rely upon heavy doses of sheer luck. One may as well hope that a tornado might whirl through a junkyard and assemble a Boeing 747, to use an analogy by astronomer Frederick Hoyle. Natural forces alone (such as rain, wind, and lightning) cannot build a structure like an airplane. Such a process requires intelligence. And what is true for human artifacts is equally true for biological organisms.

Why Fossils Can't Prove Darwinism

Three fundamental problems with appealing to fossils as evidence for Darwin's theory are often overlooked.

Fossils Cannot Prove Common Descent

Imagine digging into an ancient grave and finding two human

skeletons, one apparently a generation older than the other. Was the younger one the daughter of the older? Possibly, but she might be a niece. Or a dependent, unrelated to the older woman. Or someone buried in the same grave simply for convenience. Merely by observing the skeletons, one cannot say. Without additional evidence (such as dental, molecular, or genealogical information), the issue cannot be settled.

With fossils, we never have such additional evidence. Typically we don't have actual bones and tissues, but only rocks. Nor do we find fossils so close in time, location, and form. In the previous example we are dealing with two skeletons from the same species, found in the same location, merely a generation apart. Actual fossils are hardly ever this close.

Thus, logically speaking, even if we had a representative fossil from every single generation between, say, apes and humans—and there were no missing links whatsoever—we still could not, in principle, establish ancestor-descendant relationships from fossils alone.

In 1969, Gareth Nelson, a fossil expert from the American Museum of Natural History in New York, noted, "The idea that one can go to the fossil record and expect to empirically recover an ancestor-descendant sequence, be it of species, genera, families, or whatever, has been, and continues to be, a pernicious illusion."[12]

Henry Gee, a science writer for *Nature,* is a believer in Darwinian evolution, but he nevertheless admits that the fossil record cannot show evolutionary connections: "To take a line of fossils and claim that they represent a lineage is not a scientific hypothesis that can be tested, but an assertion that carries the same validity as a bedtime story—amusing, perhaps even instructive, but not scientific."[13]

Fossil evidence alone cannot determine ancestor-descendant relationships. Scientists draw such relationships by making what they regard as a reasonable inference from available evidence. This is known as *inference to the best explanation,* which confirms a hypothesis based on how well it explains the data under consideration. Darwinists believe the best explanation of the fossil record is common descent. But to scientists not wedded to naturalism, the fossils tell a very different story.

The File-Drawer Effect

Scientists are rewarded when they report studies showing that a widely respected theory works. They are often penalized when they report studies showing that it doesn't work. So what does the scientist whose study "doesn't work" do? Experience shows that he or she tends to just file it. This is called the file-drawer effect.

This problem has become so serious in medical science that many journals now advocate a policy that they will publish studies of the effectiveness of a drug only if all the studies, unsuccessful or otherwise, are available to the public.

To illustrate how the file-drawer effect applies to fossils, imagine you flip a coin ten times and get ten heads in a row. You may believe the coin is biased, but justifying such a conclusion depends on the number of unreported times you flipped the coin before reaching ten straight.

The file-drawer effect refers to the unsuccessful and unreported studies that pine away in a researcher's file drawer.[14] A larger file drawer indicates a larger number of unsuccessful studies that went unreported. This in turn makes any eventual claim of success unconvincing.

Even with a fair coin, after a few thousand flips, one is virtually guaranteed to flip ten heads in a row. Therefore, if your file drawer contains thousands of unreported coin flips, a report of ten heads in a row won't confirm that the coin is biased.

Similarly, for every supposedly successful reconstruction of the fossil record (like the ape-to-human progression), multitudes of unsuccessful ones are conveniently unreported and pining away in the file drawer of evolutionary biology.

The file-drawer for evolutionary biology is enormous. For example, where are the fossil intermediaries between distinct animal phyla? These should exist if Darwinism is true. Despite an extensive search of the fossil record by scientists, no such fossils have been found. As a result, we have every reason to be suspicious of using allegedly successful fossil progressions to support evolution.

Fossil Similarities Can Indicate Design

Darwinists often point to similar features across animal groups as proof of common descent. The skeletons of whales, humans, birds, and turtles, for example, have similar structures that, according to Darwin's theory, are modified from a common ancestor. But here is the catch: Similarities may make sense within an evolutionary perspective, but they also make sense from the perspective of common design.

In his 1990 book *Evolution and the Myth of Creationism,* Tim Berra used pictures of various models of Corvette cars to demonstrate how the fossil record offers proof for gradual evolutionary change (known as *descent with modification*). Berra wrote, "If you compare a 1953 and a 1954 Corvette, side by side, then a 1954 and a 1955 model, and so on, the descent with modification is overwhelmingly obvious."[15]

But Corvettes did not descend from other cars—they are designed! Different model Corvettes look similar because they derive from a common design in the mind of intelligent agents (Detroit engineers). Ironically, Berra proved the opposite of what he was trying to prove, demonstrating instead that similarities may result from common design rather than common descent.

Another point Berra sidestepped is that even though the Corvettes changed gradually over time, nothing like the massive change required by Darwinism occurred (for example, a roller skate didn't transform into tricycle, a bicycle, and then into a Corvette). At best, his example illustrates microevolution—change within a species.

Like different model Corvettes, organisms share similar features. Such similarities could be the result of Darwinian evolution, but they could also be the result of common design. The similarities alone prove neither.

Consider how such similarities make sense from the perspective of design. When people design things, such as computers, they begin with a basic concept and then adapt it to multiple ends (such as a desktop or a laptop). Rather than beginning from scratch, designers often piggyback on existing patterns and concepts that function well. A designer could therefore adapt the same feature to multiple organisms.

Fossil similarities are consistent with both evolution and intelligent design, so they cannot count as independent evidence for either one. This is another case of how background assumptions shape the interpretation of the facts.

Why the Fossil Record Points to Design

In a widely cited speech, Nobel laureate David Baltimore remarked, "Modern biology is a science of information." With the discovery of the structure of DNA in 1953, scientists began to realize how the organization of living creatures is orchestrated by genetic information. A helpful way to understand genetic information is to compare it with semantic information.

In a book, semantic information is carried in the sequence of letters. The 26 letters of the alphabet can be combined into words, sentences, chapters, books, and entire libraries of information. For example, the letters l-h-o-c-t-c-a-o-e mean nothing in the order in which they are presented here, but they can be combined to form the meaningful word *chocolate*.

Similarly, in an organism, genetic information is contained in the sequence of nucleotides, which are genetic "letters" in DNA denoted as A, C, T, and G. Thus, a sequence of nucleotides—such as GTTAGACAAGCTCG—may carry significant genetic information for the construction of a particular protein, just as letters may carry information for a particular sentence.

The connection goes deeper. Just as meaningful sentences are extremely rare among all the possible arrangements of English letters, genetic messages that encode functional proteins are extremely rare among the possible arrangements of nucleotide bases. The bottom line is this: A biological organism contains vast amounts of information that in all essentials is equivalent to semantic information carried in a book.

The emergence of biological information in the fossil record points to intelligent design. Before the Cambrian period, life consisted mostly of simple or single-celled organisms, such as bacteria and algae. Then, just as the Cambrian period was about to start, some multicellular organisms first emerge, such as sponges. And then, with the Cambrian explosion, there was a massive jump— not only in the complexity of biological organisms but also in their information content.

From the fossilized organisms found in the Cambrian sediment, we know that the Cambrian explosion was also an information explosion. For instance, sponges that existed before the Cambrian explosion would have required five types of cells, yet the organisms that emerge during the Cambrian explosion require fifty or more cell types. These multiple cell types require many new and specialized proteins, which in turn require additional genetic information.

Where did this information come from? Darwin's mechanism of natural selection cannot explain this explosion of information. The only known source for this type of information is intelligence.

Recognizing Design in Nature

Even so, Darwinists insist that natural selection acting on random variation can generate new information that leads to new organisms. Yet to create new species, new proteins are required. Given an earth several billion years old, the odds of creating even a single new protein are virtually nil.[16] And multicellular Cambrian organisms require many more proteins than the single-celled organisms of the pre-Cambrian. Could such proteins have emerged through natural selection acting on random variation in the short period of the Cambrian explosion?

In my own work, I (Bill) have mathematically estimated the point at which an improbable event becomes effectively impossible. In other words, given that our universe is finite (it has a certain size and age), we can accept only so much "luck" as an adequate explanation for certain events.

I have estimated this limit to be 1 in 10^{150} (the number 10 followed by 150 zeroes!). This means that reproducing an event with a probability smaller than 1 in 10^{150} is effectively beyond the reach of chance in our universe (think of tossing 1000 heads in a row with a fair coin).

Do you think this number may not be small enough, so that the universe can by chance reproduce such events? My probability (known as a universal probability bound) is actually the most conservative estimate in the literature. The French mathematician Emile Borel proposed a universal probability bound of 1 in 10^{50}, and the National Research Council set it at 1 in 10^{94} to ensure the security of systems that store confidential information from chance-based attacks. What hope does an attacker have of eventually breaking the code (cryptosystem) by random means? If "eventually" means not in this millennium, the attacker may want to look for a more honest line of work.

The problem for Darwinism is that the probability of the proteins emerging by Darwinian (chance-based) processes is well beyond this limit.[17] Yet these improbable proteins are exactly what we see emerging during the Cambrian explosion. Thus, we can confidently conclude that Darwin's mechanism fails to explain the Cambrian explosion and the emergence of organisms as recorded in the fossil record.

In contrast to Darwinism, the information explosion in the fossil record is not a problem for intelligent design. Why not? Ordinary experience tells us that information, such as a book or computer program, arises from a mind, such as that of an author or computer programmer. The words in a book point beyond themselves to a mind who purposefully arranged them into a meaningful sequence. Just as the information in a book points to an author and computer code points to a programmer, the information content of organisms points to an information source, an intelligent designer.

We will explore how the natural world can point beyond itself to an intelligent designer in subsequent chapters. For now, we merely want you to see how problematic the fossil record is for Darwinism and how it might be viewed from a design perspective.

FIVE

SCIENCE OR RELIGION?

GRIGORI POTEMKIN IS SAID TO HAVE FOOLED Empress Catherine II during her 1787 visit to Crimea, convincing her that its villages were thriving when they really weren't. As the story is told, Potemkin erected hollow building facades along the Dnieper River. Everything looked neat and spotless on the outside, but behind the facades there was no substance. Hence the term *Potemkin village.*

The problem today with Darwinism is the same. Everything looks neat and spotless from the outside. Museum displays, fossil finds reported in the media, and embryo drawings in textbooks all supposedly provide overwhelming evidence for evolution. Yet as we have seen in the last two chapters, this veneer of invincibility is paper thin. If we spend time scratching its surface, asking the right questions, we find that Darwinism is a poorly supported scientific theory that doesn't adequately explain the grand sweep of natural history.

You might therefore wonder, if Darwinian evolution is so poorly supported, why is the academic establishment so strongly committed to it? The answer centers on the old problem of presuppositions—having the wrong ones and letting one's view of reality be distorted by them. Consider the following illustration. Near the end of the eighteenth century, the duck-billed platypus was discovered in Australia. The platypus had fur over its entire body, was the size of a rabbit, and had webbed feet. Yet because it laid eggs, it reproduced like a reptile. When the skin of a platypus was first brought to Europe, it was greeted with amazement and disbelief. Was it a mammal or a reptile? The platypus seemed so bizarre that—despite physical evidence and the testimony of witnesses—many Londoners dismissed it as a sham.

Not until a pregnant platypus was shot and brought to London for observers to see with their own eyes did people begin to believe. Until then, people refused to accept that something like a platypus could exist. The problem, according to Ross Clifford, was that "it did not fit some people's view of how the world operated, so they rejected it and they reached their verdict even though the weight of the evidence said otherwise."[1] Many people refused to believe in the platypus not for a lack of evidence, but because of faulty presuppositions about how the world operates. Their worldview was wrong, and this in turn prevented them from seeing the truth.

The reaction of the eighteenth-century Londoners to the platypus is similar to how many people nowadays react to the evidence for intelligent design. Because they presuppose naturalism, many rule intelligent design unscientific (and therefore false) from the outset. According to philosopher Alvin Plantinga, if one accepts naturalism, evidence is powerless to refute evolution. He elaborates:

> If you reject theism in favor of naturalism, this evolutionary story is the only game in town, the only visible answer to the question: Where did all this…come from? How did it all get here? Even if the fossil record is at best spotty and at worst disconfirming, this story is the only answer on offer (from a naturalistic perspective) to these questions.[2]

Plantinga's questions raise further questions. Who makes the rules of science? Must science proceed solely by recourse to unintelligent causes? Is there a political code of scientific correctness that does not lead us to truth but rather prevents certain inquiry? The legitimacy of restricting science to naturalistic explanations is not as obvious as some would lead us to believe.

Excluding Design

In their eagerness to defeat intelligent design, Darwinists exclude ID from serious consideration by refusing to bestow on it the status of science. After claiming that Darwin adequately explained the apparent design of organisms by means of natural selection, evolutionary biologist Francisco Ayala remarked, "The origin and adaptation of organisms in their profusion and wondrous variations were thus brought into the realm of science."[3]

These words clearly suggest that before Darwin, the study of biological origins was not scientific. Additionally, because the study of biological origins before Darwin was primarily from the perspective of design, Ayala is in effect claiming that references to an intelligent designer cannot properly be considered a part of science. Philosopher of biology David Hull makes this point more starkly: "He [Darwin] dismissed it [design] not because it was an incorrect scientific explanation, but because it was not a proper scientific explanation at all."[4]

But this seems premature. Many scientific disciplines rely upon properly recognizing design. Archaeology, for instance, assumes that humans of previous generations have left physical evidence of their lives and cultures, and it presupposes that the evidence is distinguishable from the effects of blind material forces. Forensic science is based on the assumption that when people commit crimes, they often try to cover their tracks. Yet when they try to do so, they often fail, and the tracks lead back to them and not, as they would like, to natural causes. Other special sciences that require the concept of design include artificial intelligence, cryptography, and random number generation.

Some critics discount design in nature because, they claim, we have experience with only human designers. But this is not true. Animals display intelligence and can design basic things.

For example, beavers build dams that are designed. Design also need not be confined to earth. The scientific program known as the Search for Extraterrestrial Intelligence (SETI) aims to identify radio signals in outer space potentially coming from other life-forms intent on contacting us. The underlying assumption of SETI is that we can sift through naturally occurring radio signals and distinguish them from signals that are the result of intelligence.

As we have seen, a variety of scientific disciplines rely on properly recognizing when an intelligent agent has acted—even if we are unaware of the identity of the agent. Therefore, because design is already incorporated into these well-established scientific pursuits, unless we begin with a naturalistic assumption, there is no good reason to exclude intelligent design from science. Surprisingly, popular atheist Richard Dawkins agrees that intelligent design makes scientific claims about reality. In *The God Delusion,* Dawkins says that "the presence or absence of a creative super-intelligence is unequivocally a scientific question."[5] To be sure, Dawkins thinks that Darwinism offers the best explanation for the design of nature. We disagree with him on this point, but he is right that it is fundamentally a scientific dispute.

What Is Science?

In the famous Arkansas Creation Trial (*McLean v. Arkansas,* 1982), the court ruled unconstitutional a law requiring that public schools give equal treatment to creation science and evolution. The judge in the case barred creation science from the classroom because he deemed it religious and therefore not fitting for public-school science classes (citing the Constitution's First Amendment). But this begs the question, what distinguishes scientific claims from religious claims?

To justify its decision, the court attempted to list features that genuine science is supposed to have. Since then, critics of design have expanded this list of features with an eye toward excluding design from science. Here are some of the main features they cite, formulated as criticisms of ID. Note that these claims about science are not themselves scientific—they derive from extra-scientific considerations.

1. Scientific claims must deal with things that are observable, whereas the designer is unobservable.

2. Science cannot appeal to a designer because that leaves the origin of the designer unexplained.

3. Scientific claims must deal with things that are repeatable, but the designer performs unique events.

4. Scientific claims must be testable, but design is supposed to be untestable.

5. Science is limited to studying what is natural, whereas the designer is supposed to act supernaturally.

Response to criticism 1. This criticism may appear to disqualify ID, but it falls apart on closer analysis. Here is why. Science often progresses by proposing theoretical entities that have not yet been observed and may never be observed (think of quarks, black holes, and strings). Yet scientists accept these things anyway because of their value in explaining scientific data. Observability is therefore not a necessary condition for an explanation to be scientific. In addition, macroevolution has never been observed, yet it is still considered scientific.

Response to criticism 2. Richard Dawkins has been making this criticism for years now, most recently in his book *The God Delusion*. Dawkins rejects design arguments because, he claims, they don't explain the designer. *Who designed the designer?* is his catchphrase. The problem with this criticism is that it is always possible to ask for further explanation. Yet at some point scientists stop to recognize the progress they have made.

For instance, if an archaeologist uncovers an object that looks like an arrowhead or digging tool, she would be fully justified in drawing a design inference. Patterns exhibited by these artifacts would point beyond natural forces to the work of a designer even if archaeologists had no clue about the origin or identity of such a designer.

The underlying fallacy in this objection is easy to spot. If every explanation needed a further explanation, we could never explain anything! It would lead to an infinite regress of explanations. Nothing could ever be explained because every explanation would require an additional explanation. Science itself would come to a standstill!

Response to criticism 3. Science, according to this criticism, must deal exclusively with what is repeatable. But how can this be the case? Scientists study many things that are not repeatable, such as the Big Bang and the origin of life. Scientists are not even close to repeating either of these events in a laboratory, yet they are clearly within the bounds of science. If repeatability is considered a necessary condition for science, then disciplines such as archaeology, anthropology and paleontology must be excluded from science when they discover some unique artifact or feature of nature. The repeatability objection clearly fails.

Response to criticism 4. What does it mean for something to be testable? If by testable we mean that a theory should be open to new evidences and insights, then ID is most certainly testable. Darwin believed that he tested design arguments and found them inadequate. But claiming that ID has been tested and proven false creates, for the Darwinist, a catch-22: If evidence can count against a theory, it must be possible for evidence also to count in favor of a theory.

One cannot say, "Design is not testable," and then turn around and say, "Design has been tested and proven false." A hypothesis cannot be both untestable and tested. In fact, ID has been tested and confirmed across a wide range of disciplines including molecular biology, physics, and chemistry.[6]

A simple way to see that ID is testable is with the following thought experiment. Imagine what would happen if microscopic investigation revealed the words *Made by Yahweh* inscribed in every cell. (Of course, cells are not inscribed with "Made by Yahweh," but that's not the point.) We wouldn't know this unless we actually tested cells for this sign of intelligence. If ID proves false, it won't be for lack of testability.

Response to criticism 5. This criticism claims that science is limited to studying what is natural as opposed to supernatural (in other words, what is beyond nature). Unquestionably, scientists try to examine and understand things that are happening in nature. But if studying nature is the hallmark of science, then ID cannot be excluded for studying those aspects of living systems (which clearly reside in nature) that indicate design. Whether the cause of that design is located within or outside of nature (in other words, is natural or supernatural) is a secondary question to whether design exists in nature in the first place.

We are told that science studies only natural causes, but to introduce a designer is to invoke supernatural causes. This is the wrong contrast. The proper contrast is between natural causes on the one hand and intelligent causes on the other. Intelligent causes can do things that natural causes cannot. Natural causes can account for a random inkblot produced when ink spills accidentally onto a sheet of paper. But the purposeful arrangement of letters to spell "Thank God it's Friday" could only result from an intelligent agent. Similarly, natural causes can explain how the information in DNA disintegrates when removed from its cellular environment, but natural causes cannot explain how that information arose in the first place. The right explanation for that information, like the message "Thank God it's Friday," requires intelligent agency.

Methodological Naturalism

Lurking in the shadows behind these last five criticisms of ID is a wolf in sheep's clothing—an ideological weapon dressed as an innocuous rule of science. Design critics who claim that ID is not a scientific theory invoke this rule all the time. They do so not by evaluating the evidence for and logic behind ID, but by definitional fiat. In other words, critics use this rule to define science so that Darwinian evolution falls within science and intelligent design falls without. This rule is known as *methodological naturalism.*

According to methodological naturalism, science must restrict itself solely to blind natural causes working by unbroken laws of nature. Simply put, science must be confined exclusively to naturalistic explanations. This excludes intelligent design from the start. Methodological naturalists do not necessarily assume that nature is all that exists, but for the sake of scientific investigation, they say, one must only appeal to unintelligent causes.

But what justifies limiting scientific inquiry merely to blind material causes? And how do we know that empirical inquiry into the natural world can uncover only the effects of such causes and not design? The only way to answer these questions is to begin with an open mind and examine whether nature bears the marks of design. Intelligent design leaves this option open without prejudging the conclusion. Methodological naturalism, by contrast, excludes the possibility of design before any consideration of the evidence.

Eugenie Scott, director of the pro-evolution National Center for Science Education (NCSE), provides the following rationale for methodological naturalism (which she calls methodological materialism):

> Most scientists today require that science be carried out according to the rule of *methodological materialism:* to explain the natural world scientifically, scientists must restrict themselves only to material causes (to matter, energy, and their interaction). There is a practical reason for this restriction: it works. By continuing to seek natural explanations for how the world works, we have been able to find them. If supernatural explanations are allowed, they will discourage—or at least delay—the discovery of

natural explanations, and we will understand less about the universe.[7]

Thus, for Scott, science can only consider physical (material) explanations for understanding the natural world. Yet this is precisely the issue at hand—whether nature operates exclusively by blind material causes. Is there more to nature than mere interaction of matter and energy? If so, methodological naturalism will lead scientists to misread nature, which is precisely what ID is claiming.

Scott also invokes the success of science as a reason for maintaining methodological naturalism. But in that case, methodological naturalism is not a sacred principle that science must at all costs preserve. Instead, it is an optional working hypothesis that can be maintained as long as it successfully guides scientific research and should be abandoned the minute it proves unsuccessful. The success of ID is therefore reason to reject methodological naturalism.

At bottom, the problem with methodological naturalism is that it commits the logical fallacy known as *circular reasoning*, which is assuming the very thing you are trying to establish. Why should we accept methodological naturalism? Because scientific explanations have to invoke only natural causes. And why's that? Because methodological naturalism says it's so!

Well-meaning Christians sometimes commit this fallacy when they claim that the Bible is true because it says it's true. Accordingly, they reason that we can trust the Bible because it is God's Word. And how do we know it is God's Word? Because the Bible says it is!

Science Versus Religion

Design critics describe ID as religion because in our culture, science is considered the only undeniable form of knowledge. In *Kingdom Triangle*, philosopher J.P. Moreland shows how scientific naturalism is the most influential worldview in Western culture. It dominates the university, public schools, and the media. It affords scientists the right to define reality and to speak with knowledge and authority. Moreland writes, "Scientific knowledge is taken to be so vastly superior that its claims always trump the claims made by other disciplines."[8]

To see this, consider a *Newsweek* article by Geoffrey Cowley concerning happiness. Cowley wanted to know what factors help people to experience "authentic happiness." According to him, "Preachers and philosophers have always relished such questions. Now, after a century of near silence, scientists are asking them, too."[9] The article makes clear that although religion and philosophy might make some interesting observations about happiness, if we really want to understand it, we need to look to science and, in particular, to neuroscience.

Since scientists are considered the gatekeepers of knowledge in Western culture, whatever is deemed the best scientific account of a given phenomenon demands our immediate consent. This is considered a matter of intellectual honesty. Thus, to resist what is currently the best scientific theory in a given area is, in the words of Richard Dawkins, to be ignorant, stupid, insane, or possibly even wicked.[10]

Religion, on the other hand, is not seen as making knowledge claims about reality. Rather, religion is considered a matter of personal preference and subjective experience. Science, by contrast, deals with objective claims about the world. Science has given us technology—computers that work universally and antibiotics that cure infections in America and the third world. Relegating ID to any realm other than science (like religion) ensures that Darwinian evolution will remain the only respectable game in town when it comes to biological origins.

But here's the problem: Both Darwinism and ID make truth claims about the natural world. They are both live possibilities. They are mutually exclusive and exhaustive options, so only one of them can be correct. Yet instead of examining the evidence to determine which explanation is correct, Darwinists want to define science so that naturalistic evolution is the only legitimate option for explaining life.

If naturalism is correct, then intelligence is merely a survival tool given to us by an evolutionary process that favors survival and reproduction. But such a conclusion should be based on convincing evidence, not merely on definitional gerrymandering that guarantees a predetermined outcome. Clearly, another possibility is that purpose, intelligence, and design are basic features of reality.

Which possibility is right? Instead of ruling out one option ahead of time (as methodological naturalism requires), ID makes its case by examining the natural world. Researchers do science a disservice by confining it to naturalistic understandings of the world. Science should properly be defined as the search for truth about the natural world. Let the evidence speak for itself and follow it wherever it leads.

Is Darwinism the Scientific Consensus?

In 2003, Nobel Prize winning physicist Steven Weinberg testified before the Texas State Board of Education about the methods of science. He explained, "By the same standards that are used in the courts, I think it is your responsibility to judge that it is the theory of evolution through natural selection that has won general scientific acceptance. And therefore, it should be presented to students as the consensus view of science, without any alternatives being presented."[11]

In *Kitzmiller v. Dover* (2005), Judge John Jones likewise claimed that "ID has failed to gain acceptance in the scientific community." Undoubtedly, Darwinian evolution is accepted by the large majority of practicing biologists. But there is a problem with such an appeal as a reason to exclude alternative explanations: The scientific consensus has been notoriously unreliable in the past.

Consider an example from geology of how the scientific consensus was dead wrong. In the nineteenth century, the geosynclinal theory was proposed to account for the origin of mountain ranges. This theory hypothesized that massive sediment-filled depressions (called geosynclines) were slowly crushed and heated by the earth and eventually elevated to form mountain ranges. In the 1960 edition of Thomas Clark and Colin Stearn's *Geological Evolution of North America*, geosynclinal theory was considered unquestionably true:

> The geosynclinal theory is one of the great unifying principles in geology. In many ways its role in geology is similar to that of the theory of evolution, which serves to integrate the many branches of the biological sciences... Just as the doctrine of evolution is universally accepted among biologists, so also the geosynclinal origin of the major mountain systems is an established principle of geology.[12]

Whatever happened to geosynclinal theory? Within ten years of this statement it had been completely abandoned and decisively replaced with plate tectonics, which explains mountain formation through continental drift and sea-floor spreading.

This is not an isolated example in the history of science. The scientific consensus in 1500 was that the earth was at the center of the universe (Copernicus and Newton destroyed that misconception). In the mid-1700s scientists universally believed that heat was caused by a substance called phlogiston (Lavoisier destroyed that misconception). And at the turn of the twentieth century—40 years after the publication of *The Origin of Species*—the scientific consensus was to reject Darwinian evolution!

In this day, when Darwinism is so widely touted, it comes as a shock to learn that most biologists around 1900 rejected Darwin's key idea of natural selection. Darwinism only revived in the 1930s, when a handful of scientists merged Darwin's theory with Mendelian genetics to form what became known as the neo-Darwinian synthesis. The history of science is filled with such turnabouts. As ID succeeds, we can expect Darwinism's fortunes to change again, this time for the worse.

If Darwinism is the scientific consensus, it is a shrinking consensus. Dissent from Darwinism continues to grow in the scientific community. In 2001, the Discovery Institute launched the website www.dissentfromdarwin.org to encourage scientists skeptical of Darwinism to make their dissent public. Since its inception, more than 700 scientists from top universities worldwide have stepped forward and signed their names in dissent. Moreover, for every signatory of this list, tens if not hundreds more would sign it if their research and livelihoods were not threatened by challenging Darwinism (Ben Stein's documentary *Expelled: No Intelligence Allowed* makes this perfectly clear).

The very notion of "consensus science" is bogus. Speaking at Caltech, medical doctor and author Michael Crichton said it best:

> I regard consensus science as an extremely pernicious development that ought to be stopped cold in its tracks. Historically, the claim of consensus has been the first refuge of scoundrels; it is a way to avoid debate by claiming that the matter is already settled. Whenever you hear the consensus of scientists agrees on something or other, reach for your wallet, because you're being had.
>
> Let's be clear: the work of science has nothing whatever to do with consensus. Consensus is the business of politics. Science, on the contrary, requires only one investigator who happens to be right, which means that he or she has results that are verifiable by reference to the real world. In science consensus is irrelevant. What is relevant is reproducible results. The greatest scientists in history are great precisely because they broke with the consensus.
>
> There is no such thing as consensus science. If it's consensus, it isn't science. If it's science, it isn't consensus. Period.[13]

Is ID a Science-Stopper?

Skeptics regularly sound the alarm that allowing ID into science will either destroy science or severely stifle its progress. According to skeptic Michael Shermer, "The point of the [ID] movement is not to expand scientific understanding—it is to shut it down."[14]

Ironically, the truth is the exact opposite—by dogmatically excluding design from science, Darwinists themselves shut down scientific inquiry. Consider the term *junk DNA*. The term implies that because a blind evolutionary process cobbled DNA together, a lot of useless DNA should have accumulated and only limited portions should be essential to the organism. Therefore, on an evolutionary account, we expect very little functional DNA. By contrast, if DNA was designed, we would expect much of it to exhibit function.

Current research indicates that much of what was previously considered junk DNA is proving to have a function. This finding has even reached the popular press. In a *Newsweek* article, Mary Carmichael describes this changed understanding of DNA:

> Over the last decade, though, researchers have realized that this forgotten part of the genome is, in fact, profoundly important. It contains the machinery that flips the switches, manipulating much of the rest of the genome...Genes make up only 1.2 percent of our DNA. The rest of the DNA, once called 'junk DNA' was thought to be filler. Recent finds prove otherwise.[15]

Here we see design encouraging scientists to look for deeper insight into nature where Darwinian evolution discourages it. The charge that design hinders scientific progress would therefore seem to apply more to Darwinism than to design.

Is ID Religiously Motivated?

According to some critics of intelligent design, design theorists oppose Darwinism not because they are concerned for truth but because they are religiously motivated. Specifically, design theorists are supposed to fear that Darwinism destroys traditional morality. It is true that Darwinism has been used historically to undermine traditional morality, even providing the intellectual backdrop for eugenics, abortion, and racism.[16] Jonathan Wells elaborates:

> Darwinism's impact on traditional social values has not been as benign as its advocates would like us to believe. Despite the efforts of its modern defenders to distance themselves from its baleful social consequences, Darwinism's connection with eugenics, abortion, and racism is a matter of historical record. And the record is not pretty.[17]

While such implications are certainly interesting and important, design theorists oppose Darwinism on strictly scientific grounds. Design theorists reject Darwinian evolution because they have formulated a compelling scientific case that natural selection acting on random variation cannot adequately account for the diversity and complexity of life. Biochemist Michael Behe, who is a Roman Catholic and perhaps the best-known design theorist, has made it quite clear that he opposes Darwinian evolution not for religious reasons but on account of the empirical evidence.

Even if proponents of ID were motivated by religion, would that be enough to disqualify it as science? Why should motivation even be an issue? The motivation of scientists is irrelevant to the truth of their scientific theories. Steven Weinberg, whom we quoted earlier, is motivated to do science because he thinks that will destroy religion: "I hope that this [the destruction of religion] is something to which science can contribute and if it is, then I think it may be the most important contribution that we can make."[18] Weinberg's motivation is irrelevant to the merits of his science. Ditto for intelligent design and its proponents.

Is ID an Argument from Ignorance?

Sometimes referred to as the "God of the gaps" argument, the argument from ignorance is perhaps the most common objection against intelligent design. In arguments from ignorance, the lack of evidence against a proposition is used to argue for its truth. Here's a typical argument from ignorance: "Ghosts and goblins must exist because you haven't shown me that they don't exist." According to critics, design theorists argue for the truth of ID simply because design has not been shown to be false.

Ironically, however, when the evidence is fairly considered, it is the Darwinists who are arguing from ignorance. In speaking at universities, I (Bill) am frequently challenged by biology professors who inform me that just because I don't know how the evolution of complex biological systems happened doesn't mean that Darwinism is false. As I then point out, the problem is not that I am ignorant of how Darwinian evolution might have brought about such systems—*everyone* is!

In these encounters, Darwinists will often attempt to turn the tables, suggesting that ID argues from "Gee, I can't see how evolution could have done it" to the conclusion "Shucks, I guess God must have done it." But that's not what ID argues. When we examine complex biological systems, it's not just that naturalistic approaches to evolution have fallen completely flat. Additionally, we know that intelligence is able to bring about such systems. So we infer design on the basis of what we know rather than what we don't know. ID is an argument from knowledge, not ignorance.

Many biologists want to ignore the persistent problems that plague Darwinism and to pretend that the "house" of biological evolution is in order. Occasionally, though, some come clean. University of Chicago biologist James Shapiro, for instance, admits that "there are no detailed Darwinian accounts for the evolution of any fundamental biochemical or cellular system, only a variety of wishful speculations."[19] University of Iowa rhetorician David Depew likewise concedes, "I could not agree more with the claim that contemporary Darwinism lacks models that can explain the evolution of cellular pathways and the problem of the origin of life."[20]

Given the lack of evidence for the basic claims of Darwinism, it is more than fair to ask, who is being ignorant here? As we will see in subsequent chapters, there are no adequate naturalistic accounts for the origin of life, irreducibly complex structures inside cells, the information content of DNA, and the fine-tuning of the laws of physics (just to name a few!). Naturalistic causes cannot adequately account for any of these features of the universe, but intelligent design can.

SIX

THE DESIGN INFERENCE

DISNEYLAND VISITORS MUST ALL PASS by what has become a favorite place for tourists. It is a bed of flowers laid out on a sloping bank, the colors and formations of which resemble Mickey Mouse. The designers at Disneyland frequently adapt the picture on the landscape to different seasons, but one thing remains the same: Visitors unmistakably recognize the pattern as resulting from intelligent design. No one would entertain the idea, even for a moment, that such a pattern resulted by chance or from some law of nature. Design is clearly at work.

Such design inferences are a regular part of life. Imagine, for instance, that you are driving through the Black Hills of South Dakota and you encounter a massive rock formation bearing the unmistakable marks of intelligent design. As you guessed, the formation is Mount Rushmore, which bears the images of George Washington, Thomas Jefferson, Abraham Lincoln, and Theodore Roosevelt. As with the Mickey Mouse display, there is no question that Mount Rushmore was designed.

On the other hand, if you drive through northern Arizona, you'll likely come across a rock formation that is clearly not the result of intelligent design, but of wind and erosion. The formation, of course, is the Grand Canyon, a huge ravine carved out by physical forces, primarily by the flow of the Colorado River. As astonishing as the Grand Canyon is, it bears no clear marks of design.

Everyone who sees either Mount Rushmore or the picture of Mickey Mouse at Disneyland knows they were intelligently designed. We explain many everyday occurrences by appealing to design. As a teacher, I (Sean) make design inferences regularly. Was the freshman pushed by an upperclassman, or did he merely trip? Is this homework assignment independently conceived, or is it plagiarized? Some entire industries—such as forensic science, intellectual property law, and insurance claims—are devoted to drawing the distinction between accident and design. Making design inferences is a regular and necessary part of life.

The design inference is not limited to the products of human creativity. This same logic can be used to identify design in nature. In one sense, identifying design in nature is nothing new. As we saw in chapter 1, unless people are bewitched by naturalism, they typically believe the world has been designed. The apostle Paul, for example, taught that the creation reveals the designing hand of a powerful creator (Romans 1:20). Intelligent design, by providing a rigorous criterion to identify intelligently designed objects, shows that this revelation of design in nature is scientific.

The Design Inference

What does that general criterion for detecting design look like? I (Bill) have dealt with this question in considerable detail in my academic work, but the basic idea is quite simple and easily illustrated.[1] When intelligent agents act, they leave behind a characteristic trademark or signature known as *specified complexity*. By recognizing this feature, we can distinguish intelligently designed objects from those that are the result of unintelligent natural forces.

The idea of specified complexity is clearly illustrated in the 1997 science-fiction movie *Contact*. Jodie Foster stars as an agnostic astronomer named Ellie Arroway, and Matthew McConaughey stars as Palmer Joss, a theology student researching the impact of science on third-world countries. Since childhood, Ellie has been obsessed with contacting life on other planets. She wants an answer to the question, are there other civilizations in the universe? As an adult, Ellie works as a researcher on the SETI program (the Search for Extraterrestrial Intelligence), which seeks to make contact with other advanced civilizations. To make the film interesting, the SETI researchers in the movie actually had to find an extraterrestrial intelligence. The real-life SETI program, by contrast, has had no such luck.[2]

To contact other civilizations, scientists have long given up the idea of interstellar travel. The universe is simply too vast. So instead, SETI researchers monitor millions of radio signals from outer space, hoping to find a signal that bears the marks of intelligence. The real-life SETI program looks for narrow-band radio transmissions that are characteristic of those on earth. The researchers in *Contact* looked for a more flamboyant signal and found one: the sequence of prime numbers from 2 to 101 (prime numbers, such as 2, 3, 5, 7, and 11, are numbers divisible only by themselves and 1).

The SETI researchers in *Contact* took this as decisive confirmation of an extraterrestrial intelligence. They knew the signal could not have occurred by chance or necessity. What about this signal clearly indicates design? Two things. First, it's a long sequence that is hard to reproduce by chance—it's therefore complex. Note that complexity in this sense is the same as improbability (things are complex to the degree that they are hard to reproduce by chance, and they are therefore improbable). Second, besides being complex, this signal exhibits an independently given mathematical pattern—it's therefore specified.

This combination of complexity (or improbability) and specificity (or independent patterning) is called *specified complexity*. Specified complexity is a marker of intelligence. Like a fingerprint or signature, specified complexity positively identifies the activity of an intelligent agent. The crucial signal in *Contact* exhibited specified complexity.

As a mark of intelligent activity, specified complexity induces a method of design detection. This method extends well beyond the ID community. Many researchers outside the ID movement (regardless of worldview) recognize specified complexity as a valid criterion for detecting design.[3]

Specified Complexity

Complexity is the opposite of simplicity. It ensures that the object in question is not so simple that it can be readily explained by chance. Specificity is the opposite of randomness. It ensures that the object exhibits the type of pattern that could signal intelligence. The following example helps to illustrate specified complexity:

1. THETHETHETHETHETHETHETHETHETHET-HETHETHE
2. XGOENAODIWGTNHPLXCVWQIZIDLRETP-TRMNSTEJKI
3. THIS SENTENCE CONTAINS VALUABLE INFORMATION

The first group of letters has a specified pattern, but it is simple. It contains little meaningful information. The second group is complex, but it is not specified. It contains no meaningful information. The third sentence is both complex and specified. It contains lots of meaningful information. Also, by exhibiting specified complexity, it clearly signals the activity of an intelligent agent.

Complexity and specificity combine to make up specified complexity. Both must be present to elicit a design inference. Consider why complexity is so important to inferring design. Imagine SETI researchers came across a signal with the sequence of prime numbers 2, 3 and 5 (110111011111). Given just this sequence from outer space, no scientist would launch a web campaign announcing the discovery of extraterrestrial intelligence. No headline is going to read, "Extraterrestrials have mastered the first three prime numbers!"

The problem is that the sequence is too short (that is, it has too little complexity) to established that it was produced by an intelligent extraterrestrial agent. A randomly beating radio source could explain this sequence just fine. With SETI researchers monitoring millions of radio channels, this sequence is bound to come up by chance not just once but many times. But as the SETI researchers in *Contact* understood, the series of prime numbers from 2 to 101 is a different story. Such a sequence has enough complexity to rule out chance as a legitimate explanation and to point definitively beyond itself to an intelligence.

Even so, complexity alone is not enough to eliminate chance. Complex things happen by chance all the time. For instance, if you flip a penny one thousand times, you will witness in a highly complex event, and therefore one that is highly improbable to reproduce by chance. Indeed, the sequence you flip will be one in a trillion trillion trillion..., where the ellipsis needs 21 more trillions. But this sequence alone will not trigger a design inference. Why not? Though highly complex, the pattern will in all likelihood fail to exhibit specificity. Contrast this with the sequence of prime numbers from 2 to 101. This sequence not only is complex but also is specified by an independently given pattern. The SETI researcher who discovered this sequence in the movie *Contact* put it this way: "This isn't noise, this has structure."

The Explanatory Filter

The American media commonly misunderstand intelligent design as saying that some natural objects are too complex to have resulted from chance and must therefore have been designed. But this is wrong for two reasons. First, nothing is too complex to have been the result of chance. Chance produces complex things all the time. Consider, for example, a mountain adjacent to Mount Rushmore. With the piles of rocks, tree formations, and grains of sand, it is a very complex structure. But it is not specified, so it hardly meets the criterion for design.

Second, we cannot infer that something was designed merely by eliminating chance. Star-shaped ice crystals, which form on cold windows, are a case in point. They form as a matter of physical necessity simply by virtue of the properties of water. An ice crystal has an ordered structure, but it does not warrant a design inference—at least not in the same way as a Mickey Mouse landscape or Mount Rushmore. A designer may have designed the properties of water to bring about ice crystals, but such a design would be embedded in the laws of nature. The design we're interested in is more like engineering design, which looks to particular structures rather than general processes.

To determine whether something is designed, we have to eliminate both chance *and* necessity (note that necessity is often also referred to as *regularity* or *law*). In my (Bill's) 1998 book *The Design Inference,* I describe a simple three-step method for determining whether an event or object is designed, or if it is better explained as the result of chance and necessity.[4] I call it the Explanatory Filter.[5]

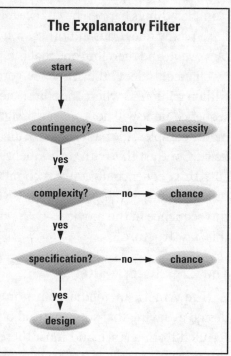

The Explanatory Filter works by feeding an object or event at the "start" node and then sending it downward step-by-step. For example, suppose we want to explain how someone opened a well-constructed bank safe. Let's assume the lock on the safe is marked with 100 numbers (00 to 99) and that five alternating turns are required to open it. With only one successful combination that can open the lock, this leaves 10 billion possible combinations.

Let's consider the first node in the Filter. It asks whether something requires (or "necessitates") the combination lock to turn to the particular combination that opens it. Clearly there is not. The event is therefore optional, or as we say, contingent; it is not necessary. So we move on to the second node, which considers whether the event is so probable that chance readily explains it. With 10 billion possibilities, only one of which successfully opens the safe, random twirling of the lock is exceedingly unlikely to open it. As any bank teller knows, opening the lock by chance is deeply improbable.

We therefore move to the third node, specification. The key question here is whether the event conforms to an independently existing pattern. The answer should be obvious—it does. Indeed, the very construction of the lock assumes a specific pattern so that only one of the 10 billion possible combinations works. This event is therefore both complex and specified, and thus exhibits design. As a result, we officially arrive at the same conclusion any sane bank teller would immediately affirm: Somebody knew and chose to dial the right combination. Intelligence was clearly involved.

Can Darwinism Explain Specified Complexity?

Imagine you came across the following sequence:

nfuijolt ju jt mjlf b xfbtfm.

What would you conclude? Your first impression might be that it is a random sequence of letters and spaces without meaning. If you see no pattern in this sequence, you have no reason to reject chance and infer design.

But suppose next that someone comes along and tells you that it is a hidden code (known as a Caesar cipher) and suggests that you move each letter one notch down the alphabet. Behold, you follow this advice and find the following message:

methinks it is like a weasel.

Even though you learned the pattern after the fact, it is still clearly the result of design rather than chance. The pattern, or specification, exists independently of the letters that form the sentence. In this case, "Methinks it is like a weasel" is a line from Shakespeare's *Hamlet*, which would on average occur in less than one out of a trillion trillion trillion trials.

Darwinists believe specified complexity in living things is best explained not through intelligence but by the Darwinian mechanism of natural selection acting on random variation. Richard Dawkins, for example, argues that this mechanism, if given enough time, will readily produce complex specified systems. That's the point of his book *Climbing Mount Improbable*. There Dawkins compares the emergence of biological complexity to climbing a mountain. He calls it Mount Improbable because it would be highly improbable to reach the top in one giant step, but through small incremental baby steps such a task may be not only possible but highly probable. Likewise, says Dawkins, evolution succeeds through a sequence of tiny manageable steps that, taken together, adequately explain away the apparent design in biology.

Dawkins's most memorable illustration of the supposed power of the Darwinian mechanism appears in an earlier book of his, *The Blind Watchmaker*. There he "evolves" the following sequence of letters by running a computer program known as an evolutionary algorithm:

wdlmnlt dtjbkwirzrezlmqco p.[6]

He instructed his computer to randomly change one letter or space at a time and then select only those modified sequences that more closely matched the target sequence:

methinks it is like a weasel.

Randomly changing letters in the initial sequence would be highly unlikely to produce this line from *Hamlet*, but Dawkins's evolutionary algorithm, by choosing sequences that matched the target more closely, did it in only 43 steps. Given the success of his demonstration, Dawkins concluded that the "belief that Darwinian evolution is 'random' is not merely false. It is the exact opposite of the truth. Chance is a minor ingredient in the Darwinian recipe, but the most important ingredient is cumulative [natural] selection which is quintessentially *non*-random."[7]

Obviously, Dawkins cheated by specifying his target in advance. The computer program did not, without intelligent guidance, produce specified complexity. The specified complexity was there all along, having been inserted by the programmer to achieve the program's goal. But Darwinian evolution is by definition blind, and therefore it cannot aim for any intended goal. At best, Dawkins's program shows that the evolutionary process is itself designed, which defeats the whole point of the program.

Monkeys Typing Shakespeare

Darwinists see time as the magic bullet for evolution. In *The Blind Watchmaker*, Dawkins invokes monkeys at a keyboard, arguing that given enough time, a monkey bashing randomly at a typewriter could eventually produce all the works of Shakespeare. Let us call this the monkey theorem.

The laws of probability guarantee that given enough time, matter, and chance, anything can happen. But how much time, matter, and chance are actually available? As early as 1913, the French mathematician Émile Borel argued that a million monkeys typing ten hours a day would be exceedingly unlikely to reproduce the books in the world's libraries.[8] The universe is very old and enormous, according to Borel, but not old and big enough for something that unlikely.

But let's narrow Borel's scope. Instead of focusing on many books, let's consider the works of Shakespeare. Here is the question: How many monkeys and how much time would be required to reproduce one of the works of Shakespeare, or even just a few lines? Let's put the question succinctly: What is the reach of time, matter, and chance?

Work has been done on this question by MIT computational quantum physicist Seth Lloyd. According to Lloyd, in the known physical universe, chance is capable of producing only 400 bits of prespecified information (this is equivalent to a string of 400 zeroes and ones).[9] This amounts to a sequence of 82 ordinary letters and spaces. Therefore, the longest initial segment of Hamlet's soliloquy that the entire universe—given its size and multibillion-year history—could by chance produce is the following two lines:

TO BE, OR NOT TO BE, THAT IS THE QUESTION.
WHETHER 'TIS NOBLER IN THE MIND TO SUFFER...

Clearly, chance is limited in its ability to explain certain features of the universe. All the chance in the known universe can't randomly type more than two lines of Shakespeare, much less an entire book. Nor does Dawkins's use of the Darwinian mechanism overcome this obstacle because it smuggles in the information it claims to get out.

Such refutations of the monkey theorem were one reason that Antony Flew—the most famous atheist in the English-speaking world before Richard Dawkins—renounced atheism in favor of a designer. After calling the monkey theorem "rubbish," Flew concluded that "it's simply absurd to suggest that the more elaborate feat of the origin of life could have been achieved by chance."[10]

Two footnotes are worth adding in all these discussion of the monkey theorem. First, let's always remember to ask where the typewriters came from. And how about the language? And whence those monkeys? Even to prove chance, the monkey theorem presupposes lots and lots of design. Second, some students and teachers at Plymouth University actually decided to put the monkeys-typing-Shakespeare theory to the test. In 2003, they placed six Sulawesi crested macaques in Paignton Zoo along with a computer and allowed them to get creative for four weeks.

The first monkey whacked the computer with a rock. Others urinated and defecated on the keyboard. In that time, the monkeys produced the equivalent of five typed pages but not a single word in the entire text. The text contained mainly strings of Ss and the occasional *A*, *L*, *M*, and *J*. The literary efforts of the six monkeys have been printed in a limited edition book entitled *Notes Toward the Complete Works of Shakespeare*.[11]

Does the Explanatory Filter Stand Up to Scrutiny?

Since I (Bill) first made the Explanatory Filter public, it has encountered much criticism in print and on the Internet. With the exception of Michael Behe's work on irreducible complexity (which we discuss next chapter), the Filter has been debated more than any other topic in ID. Such debate is both normal and expected for new scientific ideas—and it is enormously helpful for refining one's thinking. Many objections have been raised against the Filter, but we want here to respond briefly to the four most common ones. Those who want a more in-depth response to attacks on the Filter, and ID in general, can consult my book *The Design Revolution*.

Objection 1: The filter assigns merely improbable events to design. This first objection is the easiest to dispense with. Simple inspection of the Filter reveals that it can't detect design merely by identifying improbability or complexity. To get to the design node of the Filter, something has to pass not only through the complexity node but also through the specification node. The Filter therefore detects design only if something is both complex and specified—in other words, only if it exhibits specified complexity.

For example, imagine you are going to a Monday night NFL game where the stadium has 60,000 seats. Any particular seating arrangement would be extremely improbable. With 60,000 fans, any particular seating arrangement occurs with incredibly small odds. But the mere improbability of a particular seating arrangement is not enough to warrant a design inference, for if the stadium is filled, some arrangement is inevitable. Finding out that people are seated in alphabetical order, however, would definitely warrant a design inference, for in that case complexity (or improbability) and specificity (or independent patterning) combine. Here specificity consisted in the alphabetic order of names.

The biblical story of Joseph illuminates the NFL example. Joseph's brothers were astonished when he seated them according to age (Genesis 43:33). Even with just ten people seated in that particular order, they knew something was up (we might say they were tempted to draw a design inference). While ten people arranged according to age might raise suspicion, 60,000 people seated alphabetically would unmistakably warrant a design inference. A design inference results not from mere complexity (or improbability), but from the combination of complexity and specificity.

Objection 2: The Explanatory Filter mistakenly attributes design to certain regular arithmetic sequences that are associated with biological systems and that therefore have a natural explanation. For example, consider what is known as a Fibonnaci sequence, which is a mathematical progression in which each number is the sum of the two previous numbers (0, 1, 1, 2, 3, 5, 8, 13, 21, 34…). Fibonnaci sequences characterize the arrangement of leaves on the stems of certain plants. According to some critics, this undercuts the Filter because it appears to warrant a design inference (as with the sequence of prime numbers in *Contact*), but a perfectly natural process explains it.

This objection faces a problem, however. Just because a process works naturally does not mean that its origin is purely natural (that is, without intelligence). The very origin of the biological systems that display Fibonnaci behavior is itself in question. How did we get cells and organisms in the first place that could output such a pattern of numbers? A computer program could be designed to "naturally" output Fibonnaci sequences or any other specified pattern, but we would still need to know where the computer came from and how it was programmed to output such a sequence. Just as a computer program points beyond itself to a designer, so do the complex and specified biological systems that output Fibonnaci sequences.

Objection 3: Yet undiscovered explanations may account for the specified complexity in nature without recourse to intelligence.

Perhaps naturalistic explanations that we discover sometime down the road could upset the design inference. But so what? The prospect that further knowledge may overturn a design inference is a risk the Explanatory Filter gladly accepts. In fact, it is a risk common to all scientific investigation, not just intelligent design. Scientific knowledge is fallible—it may be wrong, and it may be shown to be wrong in light of further empirical evidence and theoretical insight. If the mere possibility of being wrong were enough to destroy the Filter, we would have to throw out all of science.

The fact is, certain patterns in nature mightily resist naturalistic explanations. The irreducible complexity of biological systems, the information content of DNA, the origin of life, and the fine-tuning of the laws of physics (we explore these in subsequent chapters) currently have no adequate naturalistic explanations, and none appear to be on the horizon. Just as researchers finally concluded that alchemy (turning lead into gold) was a dead end, we expect that eventually the scientific community will realize that unintelligent processes alone cannot account for the specified complexity in nature. Appeal to future theories and undiscovered explanations denies the evidence currently at hand.

Objection 4: The Filter mistakenly separates chance and necessity and therefore fails to account for their combined power. Some critics argue that chance and necessity are more effective in combination than in isolation and that the Filter isolates them by placing them at distinct nodes. In fact, the Filter does not isolate them. That's because necessity may be thought of as a special case of chance: With necessity, things happen because they must happen, and therefore happen with probability either zero or one. With chance, things happen with any probability. When the probability happens to be zero or one, chance becomes necessity. To speak of chance and necessity is a convenience. In fact, we could just make do with chance.

In line with this criticism, some critics are also concerned that the Filter mistakenly separates design from chance and necessity. For instance, is the old rusted car in your driveway the result of design? The rust and worn-down appearance are due to chance and necessity (weathering, gravity, and so on). But the car also bears the unmistakable marks of design. Chance and necessity can account for *some* features of the car, but they are incapable of accounting for other features that clearly signal design. What you get out of the Filter depends on what you put into it. Depending on the features of the car that you input, the Filter may give you chance, necessity, or design.

How Reliable Is the Explanatory Filter?

The Explanatory Filter identifies specified complexity, which in turn detects intelligent activity. We may therefore ask, how reliable is the Filter in detecting design? How confident can we be that when the Filter assigns something to design, that thing was in fact the product of an intelligent cause? The Filter faces two key challenges—from *false negatives* and from *false positives*. A false negative occurs when the Filter does not recognize as designed something that was in fact designed. It is failing to identify design when an intelligent agent was involved. A false positive occurs when the Filter assigns something to design that was not the result of design. It is attributing design when a natural explanation will do.

Let's first consider the problem of false negatives. Does the Filter ever miss design? Interestingly, both Darwinists and ID theorists recognize that false negatives are neither avoidable nor threaten the Filter. The reason is twofold. First, intelligent agents can mimic undirected natural causes, thereby making their actions indistinguishable from such unintelligent causes. Second, drawing design inferences through specified complexity requires background knowledge, which means if we don't have enough background knowledge, we may simply not be in a position to draw the inference.

Let's illustrate both points. Consider first why some unconvicted criminals get away with murder: They stage someone's death to appear like an accident even though in reality it was fully intended. Intelligent designers can hide their intentions by mimicking chance and necessity, so design sometimes goes undetected. Consider next why SETI research may so far be unsuccessful in discovering any alien intelligence: The aliens may be communicating with us in a language we don't understand. In other words, they may be sending radio signals that don't match any patterns in our background knowledge, so these signals would end up at the chance node rather than the design node of the Filter. Neither of these possibilities threatens the Filter, which makes no claims about catching every event that was designed. The Filter is a net. Occasionally designed things will slip through. The important thing is for it to catch some designed objects.

This brings us to the problem of false positives. Does the Filter ever claim design when a natural explanation will do? As a decision procedure for distinguishing necessity, chance, and design, the Filter makes its decision based on what you feed into it. Garbage in, garbage out. So if you put the wrong information into the Filter, you can expect to get out wrong answers. But if you give it accurate information, *the Filter has a 100 percent success rate in correctly recognizing design.* Substantiating this claim is straightforward: In every case where the Filter determines specified complexity to be present and where the causal history responsible for the event or object in question can be independently documented, design turns out to be present as well.

The design inference is not the product of an overactive imagination; it simply lets evidence and logic lead where they will.

A Powerful Conclusion

In *The Design Revolution,* I (Bill) posed a question worth repeating here: "Is nature complete in the sense of possessing all the capacities needed to bring about the information-rich structures that we see in the world and especially in biology? Or are there informational aspects of the world that nature alone cannot bridge but that require the guidance of an intelligence?"[12] In the context of biology, this question asks whether nature has the power within itself to produce life, and if not, what else is needed. Nature certainly provides the raw materials for life. But that's a different question. The question we are exploring is whether those raw materials alone contain the capacity to produce life.

To answer this question, it is important not to be fooled by the sheer commonness of life all around us. At one time, no single-celled or multicelled organisms existed on earth. Before that, no earth, sun, moon, or planets existed. And if modern physicists are right, there was a time before that when no stars or galaxies existed but only fundamental particles (like quarks) packed densely at inconceivably hot temperatures right after the Big Bang. Question: Was all the potential for complex living organisms, like us, present at this earliest moment in time? Certainly stars, planets, and complex life developed from this early state, but this doesn't tell us whether nature alone had sufficient creative power to produce us apart from design.

According to philosopher Holmes Rolston, humans are not invisibly present in single-celled organisms in the same way that an oak tree is secretly present in an acorn. An acorn unfolds naturally into an oak tree in a law-like pattern. But the same cannot be said for the Darwinian story that begins with the emergence of single-celled organisms and results in human beings. In no sense are humans or even simple multicelled organisms latent in single-celled organisms (as an oak is in an acorn), much less in the chemicals that make up our bodies. For Rolston, to claim that life is somehow lurking in nonliving chemicals, or that complex biological systems are already present and lurking in simple biological systems, is an "act of speculative faith."[13]

For Darwinists merely to assert that nature has such powers is not enough. They must also back it up. Somehow, from inorganic matter on the early lifeless earth, the first simple life form emerged. But even the simplest life form is exceedingly complex, needing several hundred genes in just the right combination to function properly. As we will see, even the most basic living organisms are full of specified complexity. But how did that happen? What caused it?

According to design proponents, the design of nature could not have arisen apart from intelligence. Nature exhibits design that nature alone is unable to account for. To attribute to nature the power to generate specified complexity in biological systems is like saying Scrabble pieces have the power to arrange themselves into meaningful sentences. The absurdity is apparent in the one case. It is quickly becoming apparent also in the other.

The bottom line is this: Intelligent design does not contradict the laws of nature; it merely shows that they are incomplete.

SEVEN

An Unsolved Mystery: The Origin of Life

MY (SEAN'S) FATHER OFTEN SAYS, "A problem well-defined is half solved." Once we clearly understand the task at hand, we are in a much better position to find a reasonable solution. This is usually true in relationships, politics, finances, and most other aspects of life.

So, what about the origin of life? Once we clearly understand the problem, an interesting thing happens: The problem becomes much more difficult than we previously imagined. The more we learn about life—in all its complexity and elegance—the more vexing the problem becomes.

The scientific community is unanimous that the problem of life's origin is unsolved. Harvard chemist George Whitesides remarks, "This problem is one of the big ones in science. It begins to place life, and us, in the universe. Most chemists believe, as do I, that life emerged spontaneously from mixtures of molecules in the prebiotic Earth. How? I have no idea."[1] Similarly, Colorado State cell biologist Franklin Harold admits that the origin of life is one of the "unsolved mysteries in science."[2] Harvard biologist Andy Knoll perhaps said it best:

> If we try to summarize by just saying what, at the end
> of the day, we do know about the deep history of life on

Earth, about its origin, about its formative stages that gave rise to the biology we see around us today, I think we have to admit that we're looking through a glass darkly here. We don't know how life started on this planet. We don't know exactly when it started, we don't know under what circumstances.[3]

DARWIN ON THE ORIGIN OF LIFE

Darwin never wrote a book about the origin of life. In fact, we know only one place where Darwin even commented on the origin of life, namely, in an 1871 letter to Joseph Hooker. Here's what he wrote in that letter:

> It is often said that all the conditions for the first production of a living organism are now present, which could ever have been present. But if (and oh! what a big if!) we could conceive in some warm little pond, with all sorts of ammonia and phosphoric salts, lights, heat, electricity, etc. present, that a protein compound was chemically formed ready to undergo still more complex changes, at the present day such matter would be instantly devoured or absorbed, which would not have been the case before living creatures were formed.[4]

Elaborating on this passage, origin-of-life researcher Robert Shapiro says, "This quote is often reproduced in texts and articles on the origin of life. Many workers would prefer to replace the word 'protein' with 'nucleic acid,' as we have seen. Otherwise, it is remarkably current today, which is a tribute either to his foresight or to our lack of progress."[5] Darwin wanted to find a naturalistic origin of life, but he never did, and no one since has come even close.

Without a naturalistic explanation for the origin of life, Darwin's theory of the origin of species remains fundamentally incomplete. How can a fully naturalistic theory of evolution exist without a naturalistic theory of what starts evolution, namely, the origin of life? Richard Dawkins has commented that "Darwin made it possible to be an intellectually fulfilled atheist."[6] But without a naturalistic account of the origin of life, his atheism is an article of speculative faith.

The Bewildering Complexity of Life

A *Calvin and Hobbes* cartoon illustrates how we often underestimate complexities in life. Calvin says, "Gosh, look at all the spectra that we discovered," as he shows Hobbes a pile of junk on the ground. "Let's glue them together so we can see how they fit. Then you can draw a reconstruction of the actual molecule." Calvin continues, "After that, we'll write up our findings, and get them published in a scientific journal. Then we'll win the Nobel Prize, get rich, and go on talk shows." Hobbes responds, "What about the babes? When do we get those?"

With the origin of life, the babes are a long way off. When we don't understand something, we may underestimate its complexity. We've all done that at some point. In Darwin's day, scientists knew that all life was composed of cells but they vastly underestimated the complexity of the cell. As a result, they thought the first cell might easily arise by natural forces in a "warm little pond."

Darwin lived long before the electron microscope. A cell seen under the microscopes available in his day seemed unremarkable. It looked like a confused blob without an overarching order or design. Evolutionary biologists in the late 1800s, such as Ernst Haeckel and Thomas Huxley, held that life was essentially a simple chemical substance known as *protoplasm*. In Haeckel's words, the cell was a "homogeneous globule of plasm."[7] If the cell were simply a bit of jelly enclosed by a membrane, couldn't it easily be constructed by combining simple chemicals such as carbon dioxide, oxygen, and nitrogen? Scientists of the time said yes.

Over the next few decades, however, as scientists learned more and more about the remarkable complexity of the cell, their view of life's origin had to be radically revised (as would Calvin's view when he grew up and learned that Nobel prizes are not awarded for gluing together pieces of junk). Peering through a microscope today reveals a world of bewildering technology and functional complexity far beyond what scientists imagined in the past. If naturalism did not have such a tight hold over our culture, the cell's design would be obvious.

Let's briefly look at a cell magnified one billion times. On its surface we find millions of openings, like portholes in a ship. But these are not mere portholes. They regulate the flow of materials in and out of the cell. Cells exhibit nano-engineering on a scale and sophistication that scientists have hardly begun to scratch. Francis Crick, one of the codiscoverers of DNA's structure, described the cell as "a minute factory, bustling with rapid, organized chemical activity."[8] That was in the early 1980s. Scientists now think of the cell as an automated city.

Inside the cell we find a host of raw materials maneuvered back and forth by robot-like machines all working in unison. In fact, many different objects move in perfect unison through seemingly endless conduits. The level of control in these choreographed movements is truly mind-blowing. And this is just *one* cell. In larger organisms, cells must work together for the proper function of organs such as hearts, eyes, livers, and ears, and these in turn must work together for the life of the organism.

If we peer further inside the cell, we find coils of DNA that store the information necessary to construct proteins. Proteins themselves are remarkably complex molecular systems. A typical protein is composed of a few hundred amino acids arranged in a precisely ordered sequence that then folds into a highly organized three-dimensional structure. That structure enables the protein to perform its function inside the cell.

Biologists today cannot even describe the activities inside the cell without comparing it to machines and other feats of modern engineering. The reason is that nearly every feature of our own advanced technology can be found in the cell.[9] As we carefully observe the inner workings of the cell, one thing becomes apparent: The task of designing even the most basic functions of the cell is way beyond our present abilities.

Does Nature Have a Solution?

The problem of life's origin is how to get the first cell. Scientists agree that this problem cries out for a solution. Many scientists contest that the functional complexity inside the cell points to an intelligent designer. They believe that chance and necessity can account for it. Let's therefore consider the most common strategies for explaining the complexity of the cell apart from design.

Spontaneous Generation

Just a few centuries ago, scientists widely believed that full-fledged organisms such as mice or flies could arise spontaneously, without parents, from dirty rags or rotting meat. After all, if dirty rags are left in the corner of an attic, they soon become a nest of mice. Likewise, meat left uncovered is quickly covered by maggots that turn into flies. Consequently, many concluded that animals like flies and mice could arise spontaneously—on their own and fully developed—from nonliving matter.

Despite its initial appeal, this theory is no longer taken seriously in the scientific community. Francesco Redi raised problems for spontaneous generation as long ago as 1668. Through a simple experiment, he showed that maggots develop in rotting meat not by spontaneous generation but by flies laying larvae on it.

Although Redi discredited the belief that *macro*scopic (large) organisms could arise spontaneously, many scientists continued to believe that *micro*scopic (small) organisms could do so. That is, until Louis Pasteur came along. He showed that the microscopic life forms that "mysteriously" appear spontaneously actually arrive as airborne bacteria. Instead of being spontaneously generated, these organisms are borrowed from elsewhere.

Because of the jaw-dropping complexity of living cells, spontaneous generation has been largely abandoned as an explanation for the origin of life. No instance has ever been observed, and none is expected. Australian molecular biologist Michael Denton explains: "The complexity of the simplest known type of cell is so great that it is impossible to accept that such an object could have been thrown together suddenly by some kind of freakish, vastly improbable, event. Such an occurrence would be indistinguishable from a miracle."[10]

Divide and Conquer

Even though Darwin himself focused on the origin of species, some scientists have tried to apply his ideas about evolution to the first life. Because biological systems are too complex to have arisen spontaneously, many scientists take a divide-and-conquer approach. They hope to explain the origin of life as a gradual evolution from nonliving simple chemicals to increasingly lifelike complex matter.

In 1924, Russian biochemist Alexander Oparin proposed that living cells arose gradually from nonliving matter through a sequence of chemical reactions. First, according to Oparin, gases present in the early earth's atmosphere, when pounded with energy (say, from lightning), would react to form simple organic compounds. These compounds would organize themselves into increasingly complex molecules, such as proteins. These in turn would eventually organize themselves into full-fledged cells.

This gradual evolution from raw chemicals to the first cell became known as *prebiotic* or *chemical evolution*. Except for adding a few details, Oparin's ideas about chemical evolution were essentially those of Darwin, who saw life as emerging from a "warm little pond." Chemical evolution was famously illustrated in Disney's 1940 classic *Fantasia,* in which life emerges unplanned from a sea of chemicals.

As almost everyone who has read a biology text will have heard, in 1953 Stanley Miller and Harold Urey tested Oparin's hypothesis.

They conducted an experiment that attempted to simulate the early conditions on earth. They wanted to see if the primitive atmosphere assumed by Oparin would indeed produce simple organic compounds. In their experiment, water boiled into vapor at the bottom of a flask and then passed through an apparatus, combining with ammonia, methane, and hydrogen. They then zapped the resulting mix with a 50,000-volt spark before cooling and collecting it in a trap at the bottom of the apparatus.

When Miller and Urey examined the resulting tar-like substance, they found many of the amino acids necessary for life. They concluded that Oparin was right: Life could form naturally under just the right conditions without the need for intelligence.

The scientific community was thrilled. There were many implications. We don't need God to understand life. The possibility of humans creating complex life seemed just around the corner. And yes, there *were* aliens out there. Popular astronomer Carl Sagan called this experiment "the single most significant step in convincing many scientists that life is likely to be abundant in the cosmos."[11]

Yet scientists hit major roadblocks when they dug a little deeper. For one thing, they quickly discovered that the Miller-Urey experiment did not honestly simulate conditions on the early earth. For instance, oxygen was evidently present on the early earth. But oxygen in their apparatus would have ruined the experiment. Oxygen is destructive. Think of rust. Rust is oxidation. Even though we need oxygen to live, our bodies also require many special adaptations to manage it safely.

The presence of oxygen prohibits the development of organic compounds. In the 1950s, origin-of-life researchers assumed that the early earth had very little oxygen. Yet strong geological evidence now suggests that substantial amounts of oxygen were present in the earth's earliest atmosphere (and thus at the time when life was first emerging).[12] If the gases that scientists now believe were present on the early earth are used in the correct proportion, no such amino acids are produced as in the Miller-Urey experiment. As a result, many origin-of-life researchers now dismiss the 1953 experiment on the grounds that "the early atmosphere looked nothing like the Miller-Urey simulation."[13]

The destructive effect of oxygen, however, is hardly the biggest problem confronting this experiment. Suppose it faithfully recreated conditions on the early earth and produced amino acids galore. The problem is that such experiments can't produce the right kinds of amino acids. Amino acids come in mirror images—just like your left and right hands. In fact, one kind is called left-handed (L-form) and the other right-handed (D-form). The amino acids that make up living proteins are all left-handed (L-form), but in simulations such as Miller-Urey, an equal mixture of left-handed and right-handed amino acids are formed.

To date, all natural processes known to produce amino acids produce roughly the same proportion of right- and left-handed forms. But suppose some natural process were found that could segregate the left-handed forms needed for life. If life originated by an unguided naturalistic process, how did the L-form amino acids get correctly ordered with the proper links (peptide bonds) to form proteins? The odds of getting a protein out of a soup of L-form amino acids are nil.

But suppose there is some soup that can form proteins. To form a living cell requires hundreds of distinct proteins that need to be precisely coordinated. You also need DNA, RNA, a cell membrane, and a host of other chemical compounds. To get from the Miller-Urey experiment to an actual living cell by unguided naturalistic processes requires that improbabilities be piled on improbabilities. For this reason, geneticist and outspoken atheist Massimo Pigliucci rightly concludes, "It has to be true that we really don't have a clue how life originated on Earth by natural means."[14]

Self-Organization

Given the daunting problem of explaining the origin of life, one might think that origin-of-life-researchers would be pessimistic about their prospects for a solution. But no. Many scientists are convinced that nonliving matter can organize itself into life. That is, nonliving nature has a mysterious inner capacity to produce life. Just as water organizes itself into hexagonal ice crystals, so matter is supposed to organize itself into life.

Biology professor Dean Kenyon was once a key proponent of self-organization. His 1969 book *Biochemical Predestination* was widely viewed at the time as a convincing answer to the problem of life's origin. His idea was that the secret of life lay in the forces of attraction that exist between life's basic building blocks. Stephen Meyer describes Kenyon's work this way: "Life might have been 'biochemically predestined' by the properties of attraction that exist between its chemical parts—particularly between amino acids in proteins."[15]

Shortly after the publication of *Biochemical Predestination*, however, Kenyon began to reconsider his position. One of his students gave him a published critique of the book. After pondering it for an entire summer, Kenyon renounced his position. Kenyon still saw natural forces as playing important roles in life's origin, but no longer did they seem sufficient to explain the information content in proteins and DNA. In particular, he now doubted that amino acids could arrange themselves into meaningful biological sequences on their own (any more than Scrabble pieces could arrange themselves into a meaningful sentence).

Kenyon recounts his intellectual journey in the video *Unlocking the Mystery of Life*:

> It's an enormous problem—how you could get together, in one tiny submicroscopic volume of the primitive ocean, all of the hundreds of different molecular components you would need in order for a self-replicating cycle to be established. And so my doubts about whether amino acids could order themselves into meaningful biological sequences on their own, without preexisting

genetic material being present, just reached for me the intellectual breaking point near the end of the decade of the '70s.[16]

Kenyon became convinced that the information content in biological systems could not have arisen through natural processes. He decided that the most sensible explanation was an intelligent designer. His reasoning was straightforward: Functional information is regularly observed to result from an intelligent mind, but never from unguided material processes.

Pass the Buck

Suppose you have a hole to fill. One approach is to dig a second hole and use the dirt from it to fill the first hole. But then you've got a new hole to fill. This is precisely how some theories attempt to solve the problem of life's origin. In other words, they pass the buck. *Panspermia theories,* for example, argue that life began elsewhere in the universe and was seeded on earth.

In one form of panspermia, life rode on meteorites traveling through space. Once a life-bearing meteorite landed on earth, life was here, and the Darwinian mechanism could take over. A serious difficulty with this proposal is the unlikelihood that any life form could survive the radiation and extreme temperatures found in space.

According to another version of panspermia, intelligent aliens who travel in spaceships visited earth and seeded it with the first life form. This second version, known as *directed panspermia,* may sound bizarre, but its advocates include prominent scientists, such as the codiscoverer of the double helix, Francis Crick.

Even so, just because a great scientist held a hypothesis is no reason to believe it. As Nobel laureate biologist Peter Medawar remarked,

> I cannot give any scientist of any age better advice than this: the intensity of a conviction that a hypothesis is true has no bearing on whether it is true or not. The importance

of the strength of our conviction is only to provide a proportionately strong incentive to find out if the hypothesis will stand up to critical evaluation.[17]

Crick's willingness to resort to the hypothesis of aliens tells you nothing about the credibility of the hypothesis and everything about how difficult the problem of life's origin is.

The main problem with both forms of panspermia is that they only explain how life got to earth. They don't address the actual origin of life, which is what we really want to know. All such theories merely shift the problem of the emergence of life to another location. They pass the buck.

Which Came First—The Chicken or the Egg?

Perhaps the biggest problem facing contemporary origin-of-life research is this: DNA depends on protein for proper functioning, yet protein relies upon DNA for correct sequencing. Protein cannot arise apart from DNA, yet DNA needs protein to function. So which came first? How did two separate systems arise simultaneously that rely on one another for survival and function? This is a classic chicken-and-egg problem for which no naturalistic solutions are on the horizon.

Given the difficulty of this problem, origin-of-life researchers have proposed that proteins may not have been the first building blocks of life. DNA is also a poor candidate because it relies upon proteins for its function. In recent years, scientists have proposed an "RNA first" model in which RNA acts as the precursor to both DNA and proteins. RNA is a close chemical relative of DNA that can store information like DNA and catalyze chemical reactions like a certain class of proteins known as enzymes.

According to this "RNA first" model, known as the *RNA world*, RNA might be able to synthesize itself without proteins and thus might have originated on earth before either proteins or DNA. Of all the origin-of-life scenarios out there that attempt to crack this chicken-or-egg problem, the RNA world is the one to beat.

And yet this model has grave problems. No one has been able to demonstrate how RNA might have formed on the primitive earth without living cells. And even if there were a purely naturalistic route to RNA, RNA is so unstable it could not have survived long in the conditions assumed for the early earth.

There's not a shred of evidence that the RNA world ever existed. And even if it did once exist, we know of no plausible naturalistic route from the RNA world to the DNA-protein world that characterizes life as we know it. This is why Scripps biochemist Gerald Joyce concludes, "You have to build straw man upon straw man to get to the point where RNA is a viable first biomolecule."[18]

Life's Information Problem

We have briefly surveyed some of the main strategies naturalists use to avoid the design of biological systems. Whether these approaches are used individually or in combination, they have uniformly failed to explain the origin of life. The belief that material processes alone can overcome these obstacles is an article of faith without basis. This is why origin-of-life researcher Stuart Kauffman concludes, "Anyone who tells you that he or she knows how life started on the earth some 3.45 billion years ago is a fool or a knave. Nobody knows."[19]

The problem for origin-of-life research is actually deeper than we have stated so far. When we discussed the Cambrian explosion in chapter 4, we noted that virtually all of the basic body plans for life appear on the scene in, so to speak, a geological instant. The central problem the explosion raises is therefore this: Apart from intelligent input, how could the information necessary for the different body plans of organisms emerge so suddenly?

Similarly, the first life form emerges suddenly. According to standard dating, this first emergence of life was around 4 billion years ago. For the first 500 million years, the earth was too hot and turbulent for any life form to exist. And then, shortly after the earth was cool enough, certain types of bacteria appear suddenly and abundantly.

Francis Collins, head of the Human Genome Project, put it this way: "Four billion years ago, the conditions on this planet were completely inhospitable to life as we know it; 3.85 billion years ago, life was teeming. That is a very short period—150 million years—for the assembly of macromolecules into a self-replicating form. I think even the most bold and optimistic proposals for the origin of life fall well short of achieving any real probability for that kind of event having occurred."[20]

The key feature of life is information—specified complexity (see chapter 6). Even the most simple bacterial cells teem with vast amounts of information. A single primitive cell would require hundreds of thousands of bits of information precisely sequenced in its DNA. As we saw in chapter 6, in the entire history of the universe, chance can only produce 400 bits of prespecified information, equivalent to Shakespeare's famous lines "To be or not to be, that is the question. Whether 'tis nobler in the mind to suffer." The first primitive cell is therefore far beyond the reach of chance-based mechanisms.

Because there is no evidence of simpler life forms from which bacteria could have evolved, nor even a concrete proposal for what such a simpler life form might have looked like, evolutionary biologists are left with a mystery. Here is the key question: How could nature, without intelligent guidance, take the massive informational jumps needed for life to originate? These hurdles simply cannot be cleared without information. This is why a growing number of scientists today are turning to intelligent design as the best explanation for the origin of life.

LIFE AS INFORMATION

The key to a scientific understanding of design is not theology, but information theory. If design is a part of nature, then the design is embedded in life as information. But many people are not used to thinking in terms of an immaterial quantity like information.

As G.C. Williams writes, "Information doesn't have mass or charge or length in millimeters. Likewise, matter doesn't have bytes. You can't measure so much gold in so many bytes. It doesn't have redundancy, or fidelity, or any of the other descriptors we apply to information. This dearth of shared descriptors makes matter and information two separate domains of existence, which have to be discussed separately, in their own terms."[21]

Yet the two separate domains unite in life forms, as Jacob D. Bekenstein noted in an article in *Scientific American* in 2003:

> Ask anybody what the physical world is made of, and you are likely to be told "matter and energy." Yet if we have learned anything from engineering, biology and physics, information is just as crucial an ingredient...
>
> The robot at the automobile factory is supplied with metal and plastic but can make nothing useful without copious instructions telling it which part to weld to what and so on. A ribosome in a cell in your body is supplied with amino acid building blocks and is powered by energy released by the conversion of ATP to ADP, but it can synthesize no proteins without the information brought to it from the DNA in the cell's nucleus. Likewise, a century of developments in physics has taught us that information is a crucial player in physical systems and processes.[22]

He also notes that a current trend, initiated by John A. Wheeler of Princeton University, is to regard the physical world as made of information, with energy and matter as incidentals.[23]

Information by Design

Modern biology is a science of information (see chapter 4). With the discovery of the structure of DNA in 1953, scientists came to understand that the information for organizing proteins is encoded in the four nucleotide bases, guanine (G), adenine (A), thymine (T), and cytosine (C). These four bases function as letters of an alphabet, which is why biologists commonly refer to DNA, RNA, and proteins as carriers of information. Thus, the key hurdle for origin-of-life researchers to overcome is to explain how the information (specified complexity) in living organisms could arise through material causes.

The information-storage capacity of DNA far surpasses even the most powerful electronic memory systems known today. Molecular biologist Michael Denton notes that for all the different types of organisms that have ever lived, the necessary information in their DNA for the construction of their proteins "could be held in a teaspoon and there would still be room left for all the information in every book ever written."[24] But DNA does not just store information. In combination with other cellular systems, it also processes information. So Bill Gates likens DNA to a computer program, though far more advanced than any software humans have invented.[25]

DNA sequences code for biologically significant sequences of amino acids (proteins), so we can accurately describe their coding as *messages*. In fact, a close connection exists between the information content of DNA that encodes proteins, and the sequences of alphabetic letters that convey meaning on a written page. ID theorist Stephen Meyer describes the connection this way: "Just as alphabetic letters in a written language may perform a communication function depending on their sequence, so, too, might the nucleotide bases in DNA result in the production of a functional protein molecule depending on their precise sequential arrangement."[26] Just as humans can tell the difference between nonsense and meaning, so can the cell discern the difference between a random sequence of DNA bases and a message.

This is why design best explains the information content of DNA. Imagine you are walking on the beach and notice the message "John loves Mary" inscribed in the sand. What would you conclude? You might think John, Mary, or some gossipy stranger wrote it, but it would never cross your mind to attribute it to chance, necessity, or some combination of the two. Wind, water, and sand simply do not generate meaningful information. The most reasonable inference is that it is a product of design (even if we don't know the designer). If we justifiably infer a mind behind a simple message of 15 characters, then inferring an intelligence for the origin of the cell—which requires so much more information—is fully justified.

The key challenge for origin-of-life research is to account for the vast amounts of information in living things. Even though there is currently no working naturalistic theory for the origin of life, many scientists confidently expect that a solution is at hand. By contrast, design theorists contend that without intelligence, no naturalistic mechanism can form life. On its own, nature simply does not have the power to generate the necessary information. Any scenario for the origin of life must therefore include the intelligent input of information.

Problem Solved?

A student once asked me (Sean) what I would think if scientists could create life artificially in a laboratory. "Wouldn't that be evidence for naturalism," said the student, "and disprove design?" His question surprised me. I explained that if scientists were able to create life in the lab, their work would be the product of design, not blind natural forces. The artificial creation of life in a laboratory would count as evidence for the intelligent origin of life, especially in the absence of a credible theory of life's origin by naturalistic causes.

But life—true-blue cellular life—is nowhere near to originating in a lab. So how did it actually originate? Design theorists don't know the details any better than naturalists do. The reason, however, is not that we haven't found the right set of natural forces to account for life. Rather, the reason is that the level of engineering inside the cell so far exceeds our own expertise that we are like cavemen looking at a space shuttle. Our technology needs to get a whole lot better before we can understand the details of life's origin.

In any case, to stand a realistic shot at solving the problem of life's origin, we need to be open to intelligence as the source of life's information. Design offers the most reasonable explanation for the information source behind life—a mind. This is the conclusion former atheist Antony Flew has recently come to: "The only satisfactory explanation for the origin of such 'end-directed, self-replicating' life as we see on earth is an infinitely intelligent Mind."[27]

EIGHT

PUTTING DARWIN'S THEORY TO THE TEST

IN THE 2001 FILM *THE BODY,* Antonio Banderas plays Father Matt Gutierrez, a Jesuit priest sent by the Vatican to investigate the alleged bones of Jesus. Despite the confidence Vatican officials express, Father Matt feels unqualified for this critical task. That's because he realizes if they are the bones of Christ, Christianity is false.

The evidence presented to him, as the movie unfolds, seems overwhelming. The body was buried in a rich man's tomb, with a spear wound in the rib cage, thorn marks on the skull, a coin dated to the governorship of Pontius Pilate, and unbroken legs—unusual for a victim of crucifixion but attested in the account of Jesus' death.

Matt wrestles with a crisis of faith throughout the film. Another priest, played by Derek Jacobi, doesn't even wrestle; convinced that these are the bones of Jesus, he commits suicide. Why live when one's entire life was spent following a false Messiah, one who did not rise again on the third day?

Matt eventually finds evidence that these are the bones of an early Christian martyr and not those of Jesus Himself. But the film highlights an interesting point: Christianity is a falsifiable religion. Christianity makes objective claims about the real world—claims that, by the evidence, can be either confirmed or disconfirmed.

The Lost Tomb of Jesus on Discovery Channel recently created an uproar because people realize that if the bones of Christ are found,

Christianity is false. This is consistent with what the apostle Paul said roughly 2000 years ago: "If Christ has not been raised, then our preaching is in vain, your faith also is vain…and if Christ has not been raised, your faith is worthless; you are still in your sins" (1 Corinthians 15:14,17). Some religions may make untestable claims about reality, but Christianity makes claims about real events in history that can be tested. Christianity can be tested and indeed falsified by discovering the body of Jesus.

What Could Test Darwinism?

Charles Darwin offered a test for his theory of evolution. In *On the Origin of Species* he said, "If it could be demonstrated that any complex organ existed, which could not possibly have been formed by numerous, successive, slight modifications, my theory would absolutely break down." But then he quickly added, "I can find out no such case."[1]

Darwin's theory attempts to explain how complex systems gradually emerge from simpler ones. Darwin himself famously said that "natural selection can act only by taking advantage of slight successive variations; she can never take a leap, but must advance by the shortest and slowest steps."[2] The combined mechanisms of natural selection acting on random mutation improve systems by tiny steps over long periods of time. According to the theory, such processes are supposed to explain all the complexity and diversity in the living world. Complex structures cannot simply pop into existence from thin air, for that would suggest something besides natural selection. Thus, says Darwin, if a complex structure existed that could not have been formed through "numerous, successive, slight modifications," his theory would be falsified, just as Christianity would be falsified if the bones of Christ were discovered.

In 1996, Lehigh biochemist Michael Behe published a book that showed how to test Darwin's theory. With the release of *Darwin's Black Box: The Biochemical Challenge to Evolution*, he created a firestorm in the biological community. *National Review* called it one of the most important nonfiction books of the twentieth century. Behe's claim was simple: *Complex molecular systems exist in the biological world that oppose Darwinian explanation.* In other words, he claimed to identify complex structures that are unlikely to have formed through "numerous, successive, slight modifications" as Darwin's theory asserts. Behe's claim is tantamount to finding the bones of Christ—if he's right, Darwinism is very likely wrong.

The term *black box* that appears in the title of Behe's book is used by scientists for systems whose inner workings are unknown. For me (Sean), a good example of a black box is my computer. I know how to use it, but I have no idea how it actually works. It's a black box to me. For Darwin, a black box was the cell. When he looked under a microscope, he thought he saw something quite simple, like a microscopic glob of Jell-O. As we saw clearly in chapter 7, Darwin had no idea of the cell's bewildering complexity.

Behe's point was not that Darwin's theory was completely wrong—it could explain certain ways species adapt to their environments. Rather, his point was that Darwinian evolution fails to explain the origin of the biological machines that characterize life at the molecular level. This, according to Behe, is where design can be most clearly seen.

"COULD NOT POSSIBLY"—DARWIN'S FAMOUS WIGGLE WORDS

Darwin proposed a test for his theory that is really no test at all. In *On the Origin of Species* he wrote this:

> If it could be demonstrated that any complex organ existed, which could not possibly have been formed by numerous, successive, slight modifications, my theory would absolutely break down." But then he quickly asserted, "I can find out no such case."[3]

This test, of course, could never be met, and Darwin knew it. The wiggle words are "could not possibly." To see what is at stake here, consider

Francis Crick's idea that space aliens engineered life in a distant galaxy, visited our solar system, and then left it here. Can we prove that they didn't? Of course not. All we can say is that there is no evidence that life originated that way.

When Louis Pasteur disproved spontaneous generation, he did not do so by scouring the earth and showing that spontaneous generation "could not possibly" occur anywhere at any time. Rather, he shifted the burden of proof. He showed that in general, microbes are not spontaneously generated; they descend from other microbes. The burden of proof was then on other scientists who disagreed to produce an actual case of spontaneous generation. Real science is done by determining the best explanation of the evidence, not by ruling out all other possibilities.

As a matter of fact, all naturalists believe that spontaneous generation has occurred at least once, at the origin of life on earth. Their belief is not based on evidence because no evidence exists. It is simply one of the core doctrines of naturalism.

Mousetraps and Pocket Watches

To challenge Darwin's theory, Behe introduced the concept of *irreducible complexity*. Despite its forbidding name, it's actually fairly simple to grasp, and the term now appears on television, in print, and on the Internet. Behe defined irreducible complexity as "a single system that is necessarily composed of several well-matched, interacting parts that contribute to the basic function, and where the removal of any one of the parts causes the system to effectively cease functioning."[4]

Probably the most famous example Behe used as an irreducibly complex system is the mousetrap. Standard mousetraps consist of a number of different but interdependent parts—a wooden platform, a metal hammer, a spring, a catch, and a metal bar—each of which is required for the trap to function. Now, what happens if just one of the parts is missing? Does it function 80 percent as well? No. If only one of these parts is missing, the entire mousetrap ceases to function at all. It can't catch mice. It's broken. The reason is that each of these five pieces is part of what we will call the *irreducible core*. The removal of any one part leads to the failure of the entire system.

Not every part of an irreducibly complex system need belong to its irreducible core. Consider an old-fashioned pocket watch, which tells time through a complex winding mechanism. Several parts of the watch—such as the metal case, the carrying chain, and the crystal cover—are dispensable; these parts are not absolutely necessary for the watch to function, and so they aren't part of its irreducible core. But several other parts—like the spring, the face, and the hour hand—are indispensable to the watch's functioning. If any one of these parts is missing, the watch does not work. The removal of even one such part, as Behe put it, "causes the system to effectively cease functioning."

Mousetraps and pocket watches are irreducibly complex human inventions. But are there examples of irreducibly complex *biological* systems? And if so, would these pose a significant challenge to Darwin's theory? If irreducibly complex systems do exist in biology, evolution could not produce them in one giant step because, as Darwin argued, evolution works gradually. But it also might have difficulty producing such a system through "numerous, successive, slight modifications" because any earlier, simpler system lacking the complete irreducible core would also lack the original system's function. A spring, hammer, or block of wood alone would do nothing to help catch mice. To function properly, all the parts have to be assembled in the right order, at the right time. Natural selection can only select from a system that already works. Irreducible complexity, if real in biology, would therefore put Darwin's theory to the test.

The Bacterial Flagellum

In *Darwin's Black Box,* Behe discusses several irreducibly complex systems in biology, including the intracellular transport system, blood clotting, the cilium, the bacterial flagellum, and more. For the sake of simplicity, we will discuss only the bacterial flagellum here because its structure most clearly sets out the biochemical challenge to Darwinian evolution. It is often referred to as the icon or mascot or poster child of ID. So what is it?

As we saw briefly in chapter 1, the flagellum is like an outboard motor that powers a boat through the water. It spins a whip-like tail to propel certain bacteria through their watery environments. In fact, the word *flagellum* comes from the Latin word that means to flagellate or whip. The flagellum spins at many thousands of revolutions per minute (its motor can reach 100,000 rpm) and can change its direction in a quarter turn.

In public lectures, Harvard biologist Howard Berg calls the bacterial flagellum "the most efficient machine in the universe." The flagellum is so small that scientists were unable to study it until the 1930s, after the invention of the electron microscope. The sophistication of the flagellum surpasses the most complex machines humans have created.

Like a mousetrap or pocket watch, the flagellum has multiple interdependent parts that are *each* necessary for its function. The intricate machinery of the flagellum includes a rotor, a stator, O-rings, bushings, mounting disks, a drive shaft, a propeller, a hook joint for the propeller, and an acid-powered motor. Not only are all these multiple parts absolutely essential for the operation of the flagellum, but its intricate machinery also requires the coordinated interaction of roughly 30 proteins, which in turn require about 20 proteins to direct their assembly. The absence of any one of them would cause the flagellum to cease functioning. Thus, these proteins, together with the intricate machinery (including the rotor, stator, O-rings, and other parts), form the irreducible core of the flagellum.

How did these multiple parts evolve to arrange themselves into the whole functioning flagellum through a process that operates without intelligent guidance? We know that intelligent guidance can produce such systems. But what evidence is there that Darwin's process of natural selection acting on random variation could build the flagellum, especially since many pieces, not just two or three, are required for it to work at all?

According to Darwin's theory, the bacterial flagellum had to emerge through an unguided natural process. Okay, but how? If Darwinists cannot show precisely how such systems emerge naturalistically, then on what scientific basis can they even claim that such systems evolved in the first place? If they are to be good scientists, Darwinists must construct detailed, testable models for how the bacterial flagellum can be produced through the powers inherent in nature alone. If scientists can indeed offer such detailed models, intelligent design will move toward oblivion. But without such models, Darwinian evolution is idle speculation.

At this point, prospects do not look very good for Darwinism. In my (Bill's) 2002 book *No Free Lunch*, I analyzed the structure of the bacterial flagellum so that the Explanatory Filter (see chapter 6) could start to be applied to it. Given the flagellum's numerous protein constituents and its tight specification for function, what are the odds that a chance-based mechanism (like natural selection acting on random variation) could produce it? Given all the matter and time in our universe, I calculated an astonishingly low probability of one out of 10^{1170} (which is equivalent to the probability of being dealt 190 royal flushes in a row). Darwinists have disputed this number but have offered no detailed model that diminishes it. In any case, our best mathematical estimates at this time suggest that the bacterial flagellum exhibits specified complexity (see chapter 6) and is designed.

Does Darwinian Evolution Have the Goods?

To account for irreducible complexity in biological systems, Darwinists can try one of two general strategies: direct and indirect Darwinian pathways. In a *direct* Darwinian pathway, natural selection improves on a system that performs an existing function. The system evolves, but the function (though it may adapt or improve) remains the same. Thus, a Darwinist might argue that the flagellum increased in complexity over time, but its function has remained the same, namely, propelling a bacterium through its watery environment.

The problem for direct Darwinian pathways, as we have seen, is that natural selection can only select systems with an existing function. It cannot account for how a system first achieves its function. With the Darwinian mechanism, novel function arises not from natural selection but from random variation, which is chance. Since an irreducibly complex system can only function when all the parts of its core are in place, a direct Darwinian pathway would need to assemble such a system in one fell swoop, which is far beyond the reach of chance (as Darwin himself recognized). For this reason, Darwinists fall back on *indirect* Darwinian pathways, in which both the structure and the function evolve together. Here, as an evolving structure changes, so does its function.

So how do Darwinists propose to explain the evolution of the bacterial flagellum by means of an indirect Darwinian pathway? There are two main proposals.

Borrowed Parts

One way to achieve an indirect Darwinian pathway is through *co-optation* or *co-option*. In this proposal, parts formerly targeted for functions in other systems break free and are co-opted into a novel system. As an example, consider parts selected from a motorcycle, sailboat, and freight train merging to form an airplane. Thus, the airplane would be a hodgepodge of preexisting parts originally used for different purposes. While this is certainly a *logical* possibility, it is hardly a *live* possibility. Anything that's not self-contradictory is a logical possibility. It's logically possible that you could at this very moment turn into a giant cockroach (as in the Kafka story). Our beliefs, however, need to be based on more than logical possibilities.

So is it a live possibility that an airplane could be formed from a motorcycle, sailboat, and freight train? That depends on the available parts and whether someone is clever enough to put them together to form a working airplane. But what about the bacterial flagellum? Is it a live possibility that parts targeted for widely different uses in the cell could (1) be capable of forming a flagellum and (2) arrange themselves into a flagellum without a designer? Is such a co-option scenario a convincing explanation for the existence of the bacterial flagellum? Do we have reason to believe that this explanation is true? Anybody who thinks the answer to these questions is yes is, in our view, dreaming.

One difficulty with co-option is that it can't capture the sophistication and elegance of molecular life. The bacterial flagellum, for instance, is an engineering marvel. To a first approximation, it is like an outboard motor that propels a boat around a lake. An outboard motor has multiple interdependent parts, including a propeller, an engine, and a drive shaft connecting the engine and propeller. So does a flagellum. Yet to say that an unguided material process (natural selection) formed the flagellum by co-option suggests that it is a hodgepodge of preexisting parts. This misrepresents the flagellum's tight functional integrity, which means that everything is there for a reason and is precisely adapted to everything else.

A second difficulty with co-option is that it requires multiple, coordinated changes. We're not talking about one thing evolving for a particular function, and then, without any change, getting used for a novel function. A rock might be used as a doorstop and then co-opted as a paperweight. With the flagellum, multiple protein parts from other molecular systems inside the cell all have to break free independently and join together to form a newly integrated system—and this all has to be done through a process that is wholly undirected. There is no evidence of such co-option scenarios in nature.

Furthermore, it is a dubious assumption that parts performing separate functions in separate systems could even be integrated together smoothly. Consider a bolt that's part of one system and a nut that's part of another. Unless the parts are specifically designed to fit, they are unlikely to be adapted for any useful mechanical function. This problem is even worse for the cell. In a cell, there are many other proteins besides those that are used in the construction of the flagellum. What naturalistic mechanism can guide the right proteins, and *only* the right proteins needed for a functional flagellum, to be collected and guided to the correct locations in the cell, all without interfering cross-reactions from other proteins? This would be like walking blindly through a grocery store, randomly choosing items on the rack, and hoping that what ends up in the shopping cart are the exact ingredients to make your favorite dish. Good luck!

University of Rochester biologist Allen Orr, who is not a supporter of intelligent design, states why co-option theories leave much to be desired:

> We might think that some of the parts of an irreducibly complex system evolved step by step for some other purpose and were then recruited wholesale to a new function. But this is also unlikely. You may as well hope that half your car's transmission will suddenly help out in the airbag department. Such things might happen very, very rarely, but they surely do not offer a general solution to irreducible complexity.[5]

Co-option may seem like a reasonable explanation for the flagellum, but on careful analysis, it falls apart. As we have seen throughout this book, the evidence often cited for Darwinism makes better sense from the perspective of design. This is true in the case of co-option. Here's why: The only well-documented examples that we have of successful co-option are the product of human engineering. For example, a clever electrical engineer may co-opt components from a microwave oven, a radio, and a computer screen to create a functional television. But the credit here goes not to a blind trial-and-error tinkering process (like natural selection) but to an intelligent agent who has knowledge of electrical gadgets in general and televisions in particular.

How is natural selection going to take multiple independent parts and co-opt them to form a flagellum, as our clever engineer did with a customized television? The answer is simple: It can't. The only clear examples we have of co-option come from intelligent designers. This is true for human inventions, so why is it such a stretch for the bacterial flagellum, which far surpasses human ingenuity?

Evolving Precursors

What if, instead of adapting a host of unrelated parts, an evolving system could gradually adapt an entire precursor system? For example, many Darwinists believe the type III secretory system (TTSS) is an evolutionary precursor to the bacterial flagellum.

The TTSS is a type of pump that allows certain kinds of bacteria to inject harmful proteins into host organisms. In fact, the TTSS in one bacterium, *Yersinia pestis,* is responsible for the bubonic plague, which killed one third of Europe's population in the 1300s. *Yersinia pestis* used the TTSS as its delivery system to inflict massive destruction on the human race. As it turns out, the ten or so proteins that make up the TTSS are virtually identical to proteins found in the bacterial flagellum (which contain 40 or so proteins). Given the similarities, say some Darwinists, the bacterial flagellum most likely evolved from the TTSS.

Not so fast. Suppose the TTSS could be an indirect step in the Darwinian evolution of the bacterial flagellum. This is far from an evolutionary explanation for the flagellum's origin. A detailed evolutionary path is needed from the TTSS to the flagellum. And such a detailed path presupposes that we know roughly how many intermediate systems between the TTSS and the flagellum exist, systems whose functions were neither that of a TTSS nor that of a flagellum. So how many changes in function occurred in the evolution of the TTSS to the flagellum? If the flagellum actually did evolve from the TTSS, a precise number exists to answer this question. As it is, nobody has a clue how to answer it. This indicates that the TTSS offers no insight into the evolution of the flagellum.

Ironically, the evolutionary connection between the TTSS and bacterial flagellum may be exactly the opposite of what Darwinists hoped for. If one evolved into the other, it now appears that the TTSS is more likely to have *devolved* from the flagellum rather than evolved into it.[6] By analogy, people sometimes use their car engine to stay warm, idling the car while waiting for passengers on a cold winter's night even though the engine is made to move the car. Similarly, some bacteria may have learned to use the TTSS as a pump by taking advantage of an already existing flagellum. But this is devolution, in which the much simpler TTSS devolves from the much more complicated flagellum. That's not what Darwinian evolution needs to explain. What it needs to explain is how you get complexity from simplicity. The bacterial flagellum needs about 30 *more* proteins than exist in the TTSS. Where did they come from?

In discussions about the origin of the flagellum, here is the bottom line: There are no detailed, testable, step-by-step proposals for how an indirect Darwinian pathway could produce a bacterial flagellum. Such massive holes in Darwinian thinking have prompted biologist Lynn Margulis, who is not an intelligent design supporter, to conclude, "Like a sugary snack that temporarily satisfies our appetite but deprives us of more nutritious foods, neo-Darwinism sates intellectual curiosity with abstractions bereft of actual details—whether metabolic, biochemical, ecological, or of natural history."[7]

Darwinism of the Gaps

A common move by Darwin's defenders is to claim that ID really amounts to an argument from ignorance. That is, ID is assumed to be true simply because it has not been proven false. According to critics of ID, design proponents merely capitalize on holes in contemporary Darwinism and assume that such holes provide good reason to believe in design. Darwinists believe the holes will eventually be filled in by Darwinism as scientists continue their research.

One way of stating this objection is to say, "Absence of evidence is not evidence of absence." In some cases, certainly, this is true. Suppose you are searching the house for lost keys. You are sure the keys exist. The front door of your house has a key lock. A car that requires a key to start is parked in the driveway. Well, you had better just keep looking for those keys. Darwinists believe that the same thing is true of Darwinian evolution. Search long and hard enough, say Darwinists, and you'll find the keys.

But suppose there is no car in the driveway—instead of a car, we find three tires and a seatbelt. Additionally, suppose the house has a front doorway but no door in the frame. We may be justified in suspecting that no keys will be found either. According to the evidence, this is the situation Darwinism is in today.

Current evolutionary theory has been engaged in a fruitless search for plausible indirect Darwinian pathways to explain irreducible complexity. Repeated attempts have been made to give a naturalistic account of the flagellum, yet no detailed, testable models have been produced. Aren't we therefore justified in wondering if such pathways even exist? Sometimes absence of evidence *is* evidence of absence. Remember Pasteur and spontaneous generation? We should always be on guard when the only reason for believing something is to shore up an existing theory.

The problem isn't just that you or I haven't figured out such pathways, but that no one has. And the bacterial flagellum is not the only irreducibly complex system in nature that lacks an explanation; all of them do, and many such systems have been identified so far! This problem is all-encompassing, which is why clear-thinking biologists like Frank Harold and James Shapiro (neither of whom supports ID) consider appeals to yet-undiscovered indirect Darwinian pathways "wishful speculations."[8]

Ironically, appealing to Darwinian evolution to explain irreducible complexity is itself an argument from ignorance. Despite the absence of evidence in its favor, many still assume that Darwinism can explain irreducible complexity. This is Darwinism of the gaps.

So has Michael Behe's idea of irreducible complexity been "utterly destroyed," "thoroughly discredited," and "completely demolished," as his critics claim? Behe has continually responded to his critics.[9] In the tenth anniversary edition of *Darwin's Black Box*, Behe concludes that "despite the burning motivation, and despite the enormous progress in biochemistry in the past decade at describing how life works, there have been no serious attempts to account in Darwinian terms for the examples showcased in *Darwin's Black Box*—just a few more speculative stories."[10]

Behe's most recent book, *The Edge of Evolution*, examines the effects of Darwinian evolution on tens of thousands of generations of microbes in the laboratory. The observed evolutionary changes are very small and mainly destructive. For instance, bacteria sometimes gain antibiotic resistance by junking complex equipment, much as one might sacrifice an infected finger to save one's life. Behe's latest work therefore prompts us to ask whether the gaps of Darwinism exist only in our minds (we haven't figured out how natural selection did it) or in nature (the gaps are real, and natural selection can't bridge them). Behe's latest work shows that the gaps are real and that Darwinism is powerless to close them.

DARWINIAN EVOLUTION IN THE LAB

"A normal inhabitant of the human intestinal tract, *E. coli* has also been a favorite bacterium to study in the laboratory for over a century. Its genetics and biochemistry are better understood than that of any other organism. Over the past decade *E. coli* has been the subject of the most extensive laboratory evolution study ever conducted. Duplicating about seven times a day, the bug has been grown continuously in flasks for over thirty thousand generations. Thirty thousand generations is equivalent to about a million human-years. And what has evolution wrought?

"Mostly devolution. Although some marginal details of some systems have changed, during that thirty thousand generations, the bacterium has repeatedly thrown away chunks of its genetic patrimony, including the ability to make some of the building blocks of RNA. Apparently, throwing away sophisticated but costly molecular machinery saves the bacterium energy. Nothing of remotely similar elegance has been built. The lesson of *E. coli* is that it's easier for evolution to break things than make things."[11]

MICHAEL J. BEHE

The Case for Design

Direct *and* indirect Darwinian pathways have failed to explain the emergence of the irreducibly complex biochemical machines we observe in nature, so we may fairly ask whether such systems could be the result of design. Clearly they could. Obviously, intelligent agents can produce irreducibly complex machines. So even though the individual parts of an irreducibly complex system might serve other purposes, their precise configuration is best understood as the product of intelligence.

One of Michael Behe's favorite examples for illustrating how we identify design is a cartoon from *The Far Side* by Gary Larson. The cartoon shows explorers trekking through the jungle. The leader has stepped into a loop trap and is immediately suspended in midair upside down and impaled by spikes. One of the explorers turns to another and confides, "That's why I never walk in front." The explorers immediately recognize that the trap was designed. How do they know this? The answer is simple: Multiple parts of the trap work together with great specificity to perform a function.

Whenever we come across such a highly specified system in our daily lives, whether in a mousetrap, a bicycle, or a trap in the jungle, we unflinchingly recognize that it is the product of design. What signals the design of these systems? It is that they have multiple interdependent parts working together to accomplish a task greater than its individual parts. This is true for a trap, and it is equally true for the bacterial flagellum and for irreducibly complex systems in general. Moreover, when we are able to analyze these systems mathematically, they exhibit specified complexity (see chapter 6). Irreducible and specified complexity are key signs of intelligence.

NINE

At Home in the Universe

IMAGINE YOU HAVE HIKED THROUGH THE MOUNTAINS. You come across a cabin and decide to look in to see if anyone is there. You notice that the TV is on, and it's tuned to your favorite show. On the coffee table lies the latest novel by your favorite author. The smell of your favorite meal wafts in from the kitchen. On the way in to the kitchen, you notice that the temperature has been set to 72 degrees, just as you like it. And—you can't quite resist taking a look in the fridge—it is filled with the snacks, drinks, and desserts you most enjoy. Some brand-new hiking boots—just your size—sit on the floor nearby, laced up and ready to go.

By now you have begun to notice something very peculiar: Everything seems perfectly suited to your liking; everything is fine-tuned to your preferences. Surely this is not a coincidence. Either the owner has tastes exactly like yours, which is somewhat unlikely, or the owner was expecting your arrival.

Most likely, with each new personalized discovery, you would become increasingly convinced that you are an expected guest. You might not know who expects you or why the host has prepared the place so much to your liking. But there would be little doubt that the place was prepared just for you. Given that so many factors are just right, the best explanation seems to be that someone designed this new home with you in mind.

In the past few decades, scientists have begun to realize that this scenario mirrors the universe as a whole. The universe seems to have been crafted uniquely for us. "As we look out into the universe and identify the many accidents of physics and astronomy that have worked to our benefit," says physicist Freeman J. Dyson, "it almost seems as if the universe must in some sense have known that we were coming."[1]

Recent discoveries in astronomy and cosmology have provided exceptionally powerful evidence that the world is perfectly suited for life, and human life in particular, just as the cabin above was fashioned perfectly for you. In other words, the universe is fine-tuned to support the origin and development of complex intelligent life. Many people regard such a fine-tuning argument as the most powerful evidence for intelligent design. Nobel laureate Arno Penzias puts it this way:

> Astronomy leads us to a unique event, a universe which was created out of nothing and delicately balanced to provide exactly the conditions required to support life. In the absence of an absurdly improbable accident, the observations of modern science seem to suggest an underlying, one might say, supernatural plan.[2]

The Fine-Tuned Universe

The fine-tuning argument for intelligent design begins by observing an eerie coincidence: The conditions of the universe are set precisely for the emergence and sustenance of human life. The conditions that need to be satisfied for the universe to permit human life are so remarkably exact that even very slight variations in these conditions would result in an inhospitable world. This is why British astronomer Fred Hoyle remarked, "A commonsense interpretation of the facts suggests that a super intellect has monkeyed with physics, as well as chemistry and biology, and that there are no blind forces worth speaking about in nature."[3]

Let's briefly consider three examples of cosmic fine-tuning (you can read about many more such examples in the books cited here). First, if the force of gravity were slightly larger, stars would be too hot and burn too rapidly for the formation of habitable planets that support life. On the other hand, if the force of gravity were slightly smaller, stars would be unable to produce the heavy elements necessary for life. The force of gravity must be balanced on a razor's edge for the universe to be habitable. In relation to the other forces in nature, gravity must be fine-tuned to one part in 10^{40} (that's one part in 10,000,000,000,000,000,000,000,000,000,000,000,000,000).[4]

Second, the initial expansion of the Big Bang had to be fine-tuned to a precision of one part in 10^{55}. Here's why. If the initial speed were slightly faster, the matter in the universe would have expanded too quickly and never formed into planets, stars, solar systems, and galaxies. On the other hand, if the initial speed were slightly slower, gravity would quickly force it to collapse back on itself. Either way, human life could not exist. Like Little Bear's bowl of porridge that Goldilocks enjoyed, the initial velocity of the Big Bang had to be "just right."

Third, the fundamental constants of nature—including the strong nuclear force that holds together the nucleus of an atom, the mass ratio of proton to electron, and the strength of the electromagnetic force—all have the precise values they need to make the universe habitable. Slightly change any of these constants, and we could not exist. There are 19 such universal constants that must each be perfectly fine-tuned.[5]

What happens when we try to assign a probability to the fine-tuning of these constants? Such a probability would look like $1/N$ (one over N). How big is N? Oxford physicist Roger Penrose concluded that if we jointly considered all the laws of nature that must be fine-tuned, we would be unable to write down such an enormous number because the necessary digits would be greater than the number of elementary particles in the universe.[6] This level of improbability exceeds even what we find in biological design arguments.

The evidence for design is so compelling that Paul Davies, an internationally acclaimed physicist at Arizona State University, has concluded that the bio-friendly nature of our universe looks like a "fix." He put it this way: "The cliché that 'life is balanced on a knife-edge' is a staggering understatement in this case: no knife in the universe could have an edge *that* fine."[7] No scientific explanation for the universe, says Davies, can be complete without an account for this overwhelming appearance of design.[8]

The design argument from the fine-tuning of the universe packs a punch regardless of one's views about Darwinian evolution. Even if Darwinian evolution were true, it could not account for the fine-tuning of the universe. Evolution can only proceed in a world that from the start is fine-tuned to allow the development of life. In the absence of a fine-tuned universe, not even matter or chemistry would exist, let alone planets on which life could evolve. The arguments for design from biological complexity, the information content of DNA, and the origin of life are simply additional layers on top of the argument from fine-tuning.

What Is the Best Explanation?

In *There Is a God: How the World's Most Notorious Atheist Changed His Mind,* philosopher Antony Flew makes two key observations about the fine-tuning of the universe that are relevant to our discussion.[9] First, the fine-tuning of the universe is an established fact. Life simply would not be possible if some of the laws and constants of nature had been even slightly different. There may be controversy about how to interpret fine-tuning, as we will see shortly, but the fact is well established.

Second, the fact that the laws of nature are fine-tuned for the existence of carbon-based life does not answer the question of the origin of life. These are separate matters. Fine-tuning is a necessary but not a sufficient condition for life's origin. The presence of a universe that is hospitable to life does not guarantee that complex self-directing organisms will arise and develop. Suppose we have a clear glass bowl filled with water, with small pebbles to line its bottom, and perhaps even a miniature castle or a plastic figure of an underwater diver. None of these things guarantees the arrival of goldfish. The fine-tuning of the laws of nature does not explain the origin of life. We must still account for the enormous improbability of the origin of life (as we saw in chapter 7).

The vast improbability of our finely tuned universe raises some obvious questions: Why does the force of gravity have the strength that it does? Why not another? Why are the laws of nature set as they are? Rather than any one of the infinite other possibilities, why do all the constants of nature have these precise values? These questions press on us because had these laws and constants been different, even in the most minuscule way, the universe would be unstable and wholly unable to support life—in which case we wouldn't be here.

We saw in chapter 6 that making a design inference requires a choice among three competing explanations: necessity, chance, and design. We first ask whether necessity—in this case a law of nature—can explain the fine-tuning of the universe. No such law is known. The laws of nature presuppose fine-tuning, not the other way round.

Some have objected that, as far as we know, there could be a more basic law of nature that causes the laws and forces of physics to work as they do. Philosopher of physics Robin Collins explains the problem with that assumption: "Besides being entirely speculative, the problem with postulating such a law is that it simply moves the improbability of the fine-tuning up one level, to that of the postulated physical law itself."[10]

Finding some mega-law that explains why our laws are fine-tuned would therefore only beg a further question: Why is the mega-law fine-tuned? It is like assuming that life might have originated elsewhere in the galaxy and somehow found its way to earth. That just ships the problem out of sight without solving it. It passes the buck.

No known necessity or natural law sets the laws and constants of physics to be hospitable to us, so what about chance? Given that so many factors must be just right, it is hard to believe that the universe is a cosmic accident. Physicist Lee Smolin concludes that "luck will certainly not do here. We need some rational explanation of how something this unlikely turned out to be the case."[11] Neither necessity nor chance, therefore, is a reasonable explanation for the fine-tuning of the universe. But we do know from experience that intelligent agents are capable of fine-tuning, which is why we believe intelligent design offers the best explanation of it.

Given the compelling case for design in physics, we can easily see why many scientists have embraced it over the past few decades. For instance, in the 1950s, Frederick Hoyle believed that the fine-tuning of the universe was a mere coincidence. But by the 1980s he did a complete turnabout, as is evident in the following remark: "Such properties seem to run through the fabric of the natural world like a thread of happy coincidences. But there are so many odd coincidences essential to life that some explanation seems required to account for them."[12]

Should We Be Surprised by Fine-Tuning?

A common response to the fine-tuning argument for design appeals to the *anthropic principle*. This principle states that the conditions of the universe need to be precisely set for the emergence and sustenance of human life. Stated thus, the principle is a truism. The principle becomes controversial in its interpretation. Design advocates interpret it as evidence for design. Design opponents take the opposite tack, saying we should not be surprised by the fine-tuning of the laws of nature. After all, if the universe were not fine-tuned, we would not be here to observe it.

To see why this is not a reasonable interpretation, consider the following scenario. A man comes home early from work and finds his sleazy neighbor going through the file drawers in his den. When the man demands an answer, his neighbor shrugs and replies, "Everybody's gotta be somewhere, so you shouldn't be surprised that I happen to be here." The reason the man will not accept such an answer is that he does not need to know why his neighbor needs to be somewhere. He needs to know why he is snooping in his files. What is true for this neighbor is equally true for the fine-tuning of the universe—the particular pattern of fine-tuning cannot simply be dismissed because of the general observation that we can survive only in a fine-tuned universe. We still need an explanation for why we find ourselves in a fine-tuned universe.

Philosopher John Leslie expands on this need for explanation in his famous firing-squad analogy. Suppose 50 trained sharpshooters are lined up to take your life, and they all miss. You could hardly dismiss this occurrence by saying, "If they had not missed me, then I wouldn't be here to consider the fact."[13] You should still be surprised that you are alive given the enormous unlikelihood of all the sharpshooters missing their mark.

The claim that we shouldn't be surprised to find ourselves in a fine-tuned universe does nothing to explain why our universe is fine-tuned, especially since the laws of physics might easily have been different. We agree with Paul Davies that this is an unsatisfactory explanation.[14]

More than One Universe?

Another common approach to explaining away fine-tuning is to claim that we live in merely one out of many universes—possibly infinitely many. Fine-tuning may seem improbable in our single universe. But with lots and lots of universes, the improbability would radically diminish—if not disappear. With gazillions of universes, wouldn't at least one of them be likely to be hospitable to life? If so, we should not be surprised at all to discover ourselves in a universe friendly to our existence.

If we live in an ensemble of universes, a hospitable universe could be considered the winner of a cosmic lottery, with inhospitable universes being the losers. Yes, any lottery winner is surprised at being a winner. But somebody has to be the winner, and the winner observes himself as winner and therefore is surprised. Most lottery players, on the other hand, are losers and therefore are unsurprised. Thus, chance would seem a perfectly acceptable explanation for the origin of a universe fine-tuned for human flourishing. It had to happen somewhere, so why not here? Does this throw the design inference into question?

The chief problem with this approach to fine-tuning, known as the multiverse or many-worlds hypothesis, is that we have no evidence for the existence of such worlds. None! To maintain that any universe other than our own exists is pure speculation. Precisely because they are other universes, they are not in physical contact with our universe. Thus we couldn't detect, even in principle, the existence of another universe. This is why many design proponents, and other multiverse critics, regard the multiverse explanation as driven more by philosophical considerations (for example, the need to defend naturalism) than by actual evidence.

The multiverse hypothesis has further problems. If an individual universe demands an explanation, a multiverse would seem to demand an even greater explanation. For why are the laws governing the multiverse set in such a way as to generate a hospitable world? Philosopher Antony Flew says that the multiverse hypothesis actually makes matters worse for naturalists. Consider his helpful analogy: "It seems a little like the case of the schoolboy whose teacher doesn't believe his dog ate his homework, so he replaces his version with the story that a pack of dogs—too many to count—ate his homework."[15] This is why Flew prefers design: "So multiverse or not, we still have to come to terms with the origin of the laws of nature. And the only viable explanation here is the divine Mind."[16]

The fine-tuning of the laws of physics is remarkable. But it is not the only case of fine-tuning in the cosmos. We also see remarkable fine-tuning in how well-suited earth is to support intelligent life and facilitate scientific discovery.

Our Privileged Planet

In 1543, Copernicus argued that the earth revolves around the sun. In doing so, Copernicus didn't just propose a theory about how to understand earth's orbit. Rather, he sparked an intellectual revolution about how to understand our place in the cosmos. Copernicus's legacy among today's secular scholars and scientists is known as the Copernican principle, which denies that humans or earth have any special status. As popular astronomer Carl Sagan put it, earth is a "pale blue dot" lost in space. Moreover, humans are just animals that happened to evolve big brains—brains that delude us into thinking we are special because that helps us to cooperate, survive, and reproduce.

The Copernican principle runs deep in our culture. In *The Hitchhiker's Guide to the Galaxy,* novelist Douglas Adams describes the universe's most excruciating torture device imaginable, the Total Perspective Vortex. What makes the device so horrible is that victims are forced to comprehend the vastness of the universe, and therefore, to grasp how meaningless their lives really are. Victims see a microscopic dot with the message "You Are Here" amid the enormity of the universe. The message is clear: Human life is an insignificant speck in a massive universe. Monty Python also did a song on this same theme, adding the following commentary at the end: "Makes you feel so...so insignificant."[17]

A secular understanding of the Copernican revolution is best seen in the writings of Carl Sagan, who claimed we should rethink our "posturings, our imagined self-importance, the delusion that we have some privileged position in the universe."[18] But Sagan is hardly alone. In his recent book, *God: The Failed Hypothesis,* physicist Victor Stenger claims, "It is hard to conclude that the universe was created with a special, cosmic purpose for humanity."[19]

New discoveries, however, are undermining the idea that earth is insignificant. We are learning that the vast majority of places in our universe are uninhabitable. Earth, on the other hand, has multiple conditions just right for life to flourish. The latest scientific discoveries indicate that earth is a privileged planet.

The Ingredients for Life

A cartoon from *The Far Side* shows God, depicted as an old man with white hair and a flowing robe, pulling a cake out of the oven. According to the caption, this is how God created the world. Although a cake may be a bit easier to make than a universe, there is an important analogy: Just as a cake that looks and tastes good requires certain ingredients, so too a world that supports life requires ingredients. Furthermore, just as the ingredients of a cake must be in the right place, at the right time, and in the right proportion, so too a world that supports life requires its ingredients to be in exactly the right relationships. All these conditions are perfectly met on Earth.

Clearly, a cake is the work of an intelligent designer. Are we to believe that a habitable planet, which is exceedingly more complex than a cake, is not also the result of design? Consider some physical factors that must be set precisely for the earth to be hospitable to life.[23]

Life must be in the right type of galaxy. Scientists classify galaxies into three types—elliptical, irregular, and spiral. Elliptical galaxies lack the heavy elements needed for life. Irregular galaxies have too many supernova explosions, which endanger life. Only spiral galaxies foster life, and Earth happens to be in one of them.

Life must be in the right location in the galaxy. We are situated in just the right place in the Milky Way. If we were too close to the center of the galaxy, near the black hole, harmful radiation (gamma rays and X-rays) would make life impossible. On the other hand, if we were too far out in the periphery, not enough heavy elements would be available for the construction of Earth-like planets. Earth is located in what scientists call the *galactic habitable zone.*[24]

Life must have the right type of star. A star must act as an energy source for life. But not just any star will do. The size and age of the sun uniquely enhances the Earth's habitability. Most stars are too large, too luminous, or too unstable to support life. But our sun is just right.

Life must have the right relationship to its host star. If the earth were merely 1 percent closer to the sun, then bodies of water would vaporize, destroying the possibility of life. If the earth were merely 2 percent farther from the sun, its water would freeze.[25] Earth also has a nearly circular orbit, which ensures a nearly constant distance from the sun, which in turn ensures that seasonal changes are moderate rather than severe. Earth exists in the *circumstellar habitable zone,* which is the region around a star where liquid water can exist to support life.

Life needs surrounding planets for protection. The other planets in our solar system contribute to Earth's habitability. As a huge gaseous planet more than 300 hundred times our size, Jupiter protects

Earth from incoming comets. And Mars, which is at the edge of the asteroid belt, protects Earth from incoming asteroids.

Life requires the right type of moon. If Earth did not have a moon of the right size and distance, our planet would be uninhabitable. The moon stabilizes the earth's tilt, preventing extreme temperatures and thus creating a stable, life-friendly environment. In short, without our moon, we would not be here.

Life requires the right type of planet. Planets much smaller or larger than Earth are probably less habitable. Planets must have the right core—as Earth happens to have—to undergo plate tectonics. Plate tectonics make possible the carbon cycle, which is essential for Earth to support life.

Many more factors are necessary for a planet to support life.[26] These few examples, however, show clearly that Earth is a privileged planet. But the case for design in the cosmos goes even further. Not only does Earth simultaneously satisfy multiple conditions necessary for a habitable planet, it is—amazingly—also just right for advancing scientific discovery.

Amazing Solar Eclipses

Those who have witnessed a total solar eclipse are often at a loss for words. Oftentimes, at the moment the sun becomes hidden behind the moon, crowds burst into applause. Oohs and aahs can often be heard by onlookers engrossed in the beauty and majesty of a solar eclipse.

People have witnessed solar eclipses for millennia, but only recently, with advances in astronomy, did we begin to notice a remarkable correlation: The only place in our solar system where a perfect solar eclipse can be observed happens to be the only place where there are observers. A perfect solar eclipse is one where the occluding body (the moon) perfectly covers the occluded body (the sun). In other words, the covering is exact, without overlap and without anything missing.

Even if intelligent life forms exist on other planets in our solar system, they would not be able to observe a perfect solar eclipse. Why not? For one thing, the sun and moon are two of the roundest bodies in our solar system. There are hundreds of moons in the solar system, but most moons simply could not cover the sun exactly. That would make any eclipse messy and would not allow us to scientifically investigate solar radiation, which is given off by the sun but is not part of it. Of all the places in our solar system, only on earth do the sun and moon appear the same size to observers. That's because even though the sun is approximately 400 times larger than the moon, it is roughly 400 times farther away.

Solar eclipses are not only beautiful but also have played a significant role in scientific discovery. Specifically, solar eclipses have helped scientists to confirm Einstein's general theory of relativity, they have allowed us to measure decreases in earth's rotation, and they have led us to discover helium, the second-most abundant element in the universe. Such discoveries have been the bread and butter of modern astronomy.

Designed for Discovery

In 2004, Guillermo Gonzalez and Jay Richards published their groundbreaking book, *The Privileged Planet*, in which they showed that conditions most suited for life also provide the best overall setting for making scientific discoveries. They put it this way: "In a very real sense the cosmos, our Solar System, and our exceptional planet are themselves a laboratory, and Earth is the best bench in the lab."[27] In short, our planet is not merely fine-tuned for life; it is also fine-tuned for discovery.

Imagine again that you are a hiker, but this time you are exploring a high, barren mountain in Hawaii. Unknown to you, it happens to be Mauna Kea, home of the famous Keck telescopes. Although you may have been hoping to enjoy the sunset alone, when you finally reach the top and discover the telescopes, you would likely not be surprised to find them perched atop this mountain rather than in, say, the center of Honolulu. Why not? The reason is simple:

Astronomers place telescopes where the conditions for viewing are most favorable. Telescopes don't exist on mountaintops by chance or by some law of nature—they're put there by design. Earth is much like a telescope on top of a mountain—it's located where viewing conditions are best.

Perfect solar eclipses provide just one example that Gonzalez and Richards consider in *The Privileged Planet* to show that earth is just right not only for life but also for discovery. Consider some other examples:

- Our galaxy, the Milky Way, is a spiral galaxy, which —in addition to being the only kind of galaxy able to support life—is relatively flat. As a consequence, it has less gas and dust than others and fewer stars to impede our view of the rest of the universe.

- Earth is located not only in the galactic habitable zone but also in the right place where minimal light pollution and other visual obstructions might impede the view of our surroundings. In addition, Earth's atmosphere, which is the only one we know of that can support life, is also the only one clear enough to allow us to observe the universe.

Over and over again, the very conditions that make life possible are also the conditions enabling scientific discovery. In light of this relationship between habitability and discovery, Gonzalez concludes, "The universe was designed for observers living in places where they can make scientific discoveries...There may be other purposes to the universe, but at least we know that scientific discovery was one of them."[28]

This fact is deeply surprising for naturalists, who see us and our place in the cosmos as accidents of natural history. But it makes a lot of sense to theists, who see us and our place in the cosmos as fully intended by a wise and benevolent creator. Jews and Christians have long believed that, in addition to revealing Himself in the book of

Scripture, God reveals Himself in nature. The psalmist put it this way: "The heavens declare the glory of God; the skies proclaim the work of his hands. Day after day they pour forth speech; night after night they display knowledge."[29]

Where Did the Big Bang Come From?

In a well-known joke, a group of scientists approach God and claim they can do everything He can. "Like what?" asks God. "Like creating human beings," say the scientists. "Show me," says God. The scientists say, "Well, we start with some dust, and then—" God interrupts, "Wait a second. Get your own dust." Just as a carpenter must use preexisting wood to build a cabinet, so these scientists relied on preexisting dust to create a human being.

But where did the dust come from? From stars? And where did the stars come from? From the Big Bang? And where did the Big Bang come from? From a quantum vacuum fluctuation? In a quantum vacuum fluctuation, the universe is supposed to create itself out of nothing simply by dividing from nothing into positive and negative energy (which cancel out to form nothing). So where did a quantum vacuum fluctuation that's able to divide itself into positive and negative energy come from? At some point such questions must end at an ultimate reality—the source of being of the universe.

For millennia, atheists claimed that the universe alone is eternal, which would mean that it is largely static and uniform. Theists countered that God is the ultimate cause of the world and that He alone is infinite and eternal. Scientifically speaking, there seemed no way to judge who was right. But this began to change in the early part of the twentieth century when Einstein developed his general theory of relativity. His equations strongly suggested that the universe was not static, but that it was either expanding or contracting.

Though not an atheist, Einstein was deeply irritated by the theistic implications of his findings. A start to the universe seems to imply a starter. Consequently, Einstein adjusted his theory to allow for an eternal universe by introducing the most famous fudge factor for an eternal universe by introducing the most famous fudge factor of all time, his *cosmological constant*. Einstein, of course, wasn't alone in trying to jerry-rig science to support an eternal universe. Many scientists have been bothered by the implications of the Big Bang and, as a result, have worked very hard to find a scientifically credible way for the universe to be eternal or even multiple.[30]

Einstein Repents

Why did Einstein change his mind? Edwin Hubble, the legendary cosmologist, made a discovery that prompted Einstein to reevaluate his findings. With the latest telescopes of his day, Hubble was able to observe galaxies never seen before, and through a phenomenon called the *red-shift*, he noticed that the universe was expanding in all directions.

The implication was clear: If we could rewind time, we would see the universe shrinking back to a single origin, marking the beginning of time, space, and matter itself. The universe did not appear to be infinite or eternal. A simple extrapolation form the universe's present rate of expansion implied that the universe burst into existence 13.8 billion years ago. After hearing about Hubble's findings, Einstein visited him in California to see the evidence for himself. Hubble quickly convinced Einstein that we live in an expanding universe. Einstein subsequently referred to his jerry-rigging of relativity theory to support a static (eternal) universe as the greatest blunder of his career.

If the universe is expanding, then going backward in time, it is contracting. If we take the contraction as far back as it will go, we reach a point of maximal contraction. If we now run the videotape of the universe forward, we witness a cosmic explosion known as the Big Bang. Many scientists now think of the universe as originating in such an explosion.

While details about the Big Bang continue to be debated, the scientific community as a whole, and many ID scientists in particular, think that our universe had a beginning of this type. This remarkable finding offers stunning confirmation for the book of Genesis, which posits a beginning to the universe. This is why Nobel laureate Arno Penzias declared, "The best data we have are exactly what I would have predicted had I nothing to go on but the five books of Moses, the Psalms, and the Bible as a whole."[31]

In *Darwin Strikes Back,* Thomas Woodward makes two important observations about the acceptance of the Big Bang.[32] First, while the Big Bang may have religious implications, that was not enough to warrant its rejection. It eventually earned a fair hearing from the scientific establishment on its merits—though we should note that the process took about 40 years. As we saw in chapter 2, the key issue is not whether a theory has religious or antireligious implications, but whether we have good reasons to believe it is true. The same is true with ID: It may have religious implications, but that is not a good reason to exclude it from scientific consideration.

Second, the Big Bang was one of the first modern scientific findings to challenge naturalism. It did this by providing evidence against naturalism's claim that the world is eternal. If the universe has no beginning, no cause is required. But if it has a beginning, we can reasonably believe that a designer brought it into existence.[33]

In *God and the Astronomers,* agnostic astronomer Robert Jastrow considers whether the Big Bang points toward a designer of the universe. He closed his book with these famous words, which also seem an appropriate conclusion to this chapter: "For the scientist who has lived by his faith in the power of reason, the story ends like a bad dream. He has scaled the mountains of ignorance; he is about to conquer the highest peak; as he pulls himself over the final rock, he is greeted by a band of theologians who have been sitting there for centuries."[34]

TEN

JOINING THE DESIGN REVOLUTION

NINTENDO REVOLUTION. Revolution Studios. New England Revolution. Revolution Health. Snowboard Revolution. Then there's the sexual revolution, the Internet revolution, and the communications revolution. Today, everybody's talking revolution. No wonder we become jaded and skeptical. After all, how many *real* revolutions can take place in a lifetime?

But real revolutions do happen. There is good reason to believe that design will revolutionize science and our conception of the world. Does this strike you as overly optimistic? After all, Darwinism is accepted by an impressive majority of scientists worldwide. Could it really be overturned in our lifetime? Such things happen.

Recall the geosynclinal theory from chapter 5. It was widely considered to be the best explanation for the formation of mountain ranges. Then plate tectonics came along and completely replaced it. This is not an isolated event in the history of science. Firmly held scientific theories often get significantly modified and sometimes completely overturned. Einstein led a scientific revolution, as did Copernicus, Newton, Maxwell, Boltzmann, and Heisenberg. They all invented radically new ways of thinking about the natural world.

And let's not forget Darwin. With the release of his *Origin of Species* in 1859, Darwin revolutionized science. He offered a powerful vision for understanding biology that eliminated design and that demoted us from creatures made in the image of God to mere animals.

But Darwinism has run its course. Design is now revolutionizing the way we see the world, much as Darwinism did more than a century ago. According to communication theorist Thomas Woodward, "We have arrived at the historical tipping point…In coming years, more than at any time in its previous history of a century and a half, college and university graduates across the world will begin to doubt that the fantastic claims of Darwinism about the complexity-building powers of nature are really resting on sound evidence and careful testing."[1] Woodward sees this debate skyrocketing in coming years.

Scientific Revolutions

In *The Structure of Scientific Revolutions,* philosopher of science Thomas Kuhn shows that science does not progress simply by adding one discovery to another. It often undergoes what he calls *paradigm shifts.* These are radical changes in the theories that the scientific community accepts. Sometimes the changes are so radical that an old theory is completely abandoned—it becomes regarded as so wrong that hardly anything from it can be salvaged.

We disagree with Kuhn's view that theory-change in science is irrational (he compares it to a religious conversion), but he made three important points about scientific revolutions that are relevant to the debate between Darwinism and ID:

- At the heart of a scientific revolution is the definition of science. What makes something scientific? Who defines the rules?
- Scientific revolutions often play out like political revolutions: One party defends the status quo, and the other challenges it.
- Scientific revolutions are typically advanced by either

younger scientists or those outside the field without the baggage of the old paradigm.

All three of these points are true for the design revolution, but the last point especially interests us. In his *Politically Incorrect Guide to Darwinism and Intelligent Design,* Jonathan Wells develops it further: "The outcome of this scientific revolution will be decided by young people who have the courage to question dogmatism and follow the evidence wherever it leads."[2] Many young people today realize how incredibly high the stakes are in the debate over Darwinism and design. Without design, we are left with not only no God but also no objective basis for morality, no free will, and no life beyond this life.

Young people are now increasingly embracing intelligent design and using it to unseat Darwinism. Like former atheist Antony Flew, they are willing to follow the evidence wherever it leads. They understand that intelligent design is inciting a revolution. And they want to get involved.

An especially significant sign that interest in ID is growing among young people is the explosive growth of IDEA student clubs (Intelligent Design and Evolution Awareness—www.ideacenter.org). The first of these clubs began a few years ago at the San Diego campus of the University of California. At the time of this writing, there are now 35 clubs on high school and college campuses across the United States and as far as the Ukraine, Canada, Kenya, and the Philippines. Students start these clubs on their campuses to promote the scientific case for design through friendly, informal, and informed exchanges with fellow students and faculty.

As exciting as such developments are, we should not get starry-eyed. Thomas Kuhn also taught us that scientific revolutions are not won by winning representatives of the old guard, who rarely change their minds. As Kuhn describes them, scientific revolutions are won grave by grave as the old guard dies off and a new generation comes to replace it. That generation includes you, the reader of this book!

Why doesn't the old guard accept the new paradigm? By being wedded to a failing paradigm, they suffer from the misconceptions, blind spots, and prejudices that always infect a dying way of thought. As attorney Edward Sisson points out in a book I (Bill) edited, "A psychology I see every day in litigation is that opposing lawyers are primed to reject every statement by the other side because there is no advantage to considering that the statements might be true. I also see that psychology again and again within institutional science in the debate over the origin and subsequent diversification of life."[3]

THE SINCERITY RULE IN SCIENCE

In litigation, even if a lawyer does develop an internal belief about the data that conflicts with the presentation he or she needs to make in court, the lawyer is expected to keep that belief private. The lawyer's obligation is not actually to *be* sincere but to *appear* sincere. Thus there is no danger to the lawyer's livelihood if the lawyer develops a private understanding of the data that conflicts with the understanding to be presented in court.

But in science the rule is different. Scientists are actually supposed to be sincere. They are supposed to develop genuine, individual opinions about the data and then express those opinions. Thus it is vital to a scientist's career not to develop opinions which, if expressed, will end that career. Opinions once developed are supposed to be expressed, not hidden in favor of expressing opinions the scientist does not sincerely believe. We may call this the *sincerity rule* for short.

As a practical matter, no one who has risen to the leadership of a major American scientific institution can publicly abandon the paradigm of unintelligent evolution. Censorship, removal from office (unless there's tenure), vanishing of research funds, and ostracism would be sure to follow. Thus researchers are prohibited from taking the time to consider the challenges to the paradigm and to develop an individual response because if that response is a rejection of the paradigm, the scientist must either suppress it (and violate the rule that scientists should be sincere) or else express it (and likely end his or her career).

Everyone below on the hierarchy ladder knows that to question unintelligent evolution will mean the end of career advancement. So they also have no incentive to consider that the challenges to unintelligent evolution might be valid. To the contrary, they have very strong incentives *not* to consider those challenges in any way that might lead to an acceptance of those challenges.

The sincerity rule means that if scientists develop a disbelief in unintelligent evolution, they must express it. Thus, preservation of career advancement opportunities is predicated on the maintenance of belief in unintelligent evolution. That is why challenges to the theory of evolution at best will receive a condescending hearing controlled by persons primed and motivated in every instance to reject those challenges.[4]

I [Bill] have witnessed this psychology in the attacks on my own work and that of my colleagues. By any objective standards, the principal players in the ID movement are well-educated and smart. Phillip Johnson, for instance, graduated first in his law school class at the University of Chicago and clerked for Chief Justice Earl Warren. Ben Stein graduated first in his law school class at Yale. Jonathan Wells scored double 800s on his SATs and was awarded a full, merit-based undergraduate scholarship at Princeton in the 1960s. Guillermo Gonzalez, as a young assistant professor starting at Iowa State University, had more than 60 articles in refereed astronomy and astrophysical journals—and Iowa State still denied him tenure (see his story in *Expelled: No Intelligence Allowed*).

Even so, when critics evaluate our work on intelligent design, we never seem to get anything right. You'd think that somewhere, somehow we might make a valid point critical of evolutionary theory. You'd think that no scientific theory could be so flawless as evolution's defenders make out. But no, the design community is completely out to lunch when it criticizes Darwinian evolution.

The reaction by Darwinists to Jonathan Wells's *Icons of Evolution* exemplifies this unwillingness to concede anything to intelligent design. In that book, Wells analyzes ten "icons of evolution." The reason for calling them icons is that they are presented in high school and college biology textbooks as slam-dunk evidence for evolutionary theory. Included are the Haeckel embryo drawings, the Miller-Urey experiment, and changes in coloration of the peppered moth. In every instance, when these icons are carefully examined, they do not support Darwinian evolution.

What has been the response of the evolutionary community? To issue an apology for misleading our young people? To fix the mistakes in the textbooks? No, but to cast Jonathan Wells as a lunatic. Go to the National Center of Science Education website (the premier pro-evolution lobby group), and you'll find no admission that any of these icons pose a problem for evolutionary theory or should be corrected in the textbooks. Rather, the fault is said to lie with Wells for inventing problems where none exist.

In fact, Eugenie Scott, the head of the National Center for Science Education, insists on maintaining the illusion that everything is fine with textbook treatments of evolution. Her rationale? To do otherwise is to "confuse kids about the soundness of evolution as a science."[5] Whatever happened to science education nurturing the capacity of young minds for critical thought? Whatever happened to exposing students to as much information as required to form balanced scientific judgments?

Scientific revolutions are nasty affairs. They impact everything from fundamental scientific research to science education. If you don't like the sight of blood, better to stay away.

Counting the Cost

If there are career disincentives for challenging Darwinism, there are career incentives for attacking intelligent design and its proponents. Take Judge John E. Jones III. He ruled at the 2005 *Kitzmiller v. Dover* trial that intelligent design was religion. In his ruling, he copied verbatim from the ACLU playbook.[6] What was his reward for giving intelligent design a black eye? *Time* magazine voted him one of its 100 most influential people of 2005, *Wired* magazine voted him one of its 10 "sexiest geeks" of 2005, and several colleges awarded him honorary doctorates.

So beware, you become a target the instant you support intelligent design. As Ben Stein's movie *Expelled* makes clear, there is a big price to be paid for challenging Darwinism. Scientists and teachers who have dared to question Darwinism have had their careers, livelihoods, and reputations assaulted and, in some cases, ruined (I [Bill] write from personal experience). Do an online search and see for yourself. This is why Michael Behe gave the following advice to graduate students in an interview for *The Harvard Political Review*: "There's good reason to be afraid. Even if you're not fired from your job, you will easily be passed over for promotions. I would strongly advise graduate students who are skeptical of Darwinian theory not to make their views known."[7]

Behe's advice is prudent if you need to get through school so you can take on Darwinian naturalism later once you are in a stronger position to do so. But in this controversy, you must take a stand sometime, and what will you do then? Our calling as Christians is to bear witness to the truth, both the truth of God's work in Christ and the truth of God's work in creation. Moreover, Christian witness is always a witness unto death, be it the death of our bodies or the death of our careers. The church has a name for this—martyrdom. The early church considered martyrdom the highest Christian calling. Martyrdom was counted an honor and privilege, a way of sharing in Christ's sufferings and living out the Christian life in its most logical and complete form.

Our Christian witness about God's work in creation is a call to martyrdom. Perhaps not a martyrdom where we spill our blood (although that too may be required), but a martyrdom where we witness to the truth without being concerned about our careers, political correctness, the current fashion, or toeing the party line.

We are not called to please the world. We are called to proclaim the truth to the world.

Although the evolution versus ID controversy often feels like a fight to the finish, it's important to keep our sense of humor and realize we are playing the winning hand. Evolutionary theory is essentially a relic of failed nineteenth-century economic theories about competition for scarce resources. We, on the other hand, live in the twenty-first century, in an age when information is limitless and freely created. And ID is a theory of information. Despite all the protestations by Darwinists that ID is unscientific, ID is the cutting edge in science.

Another advantage we have is that we can admit our mistakes and receive instruction. The evolutionists cannot. Indeed, the moment they admit that we might have a point, they let the genie out of the bottle. To open evolutionary theory to critical scrutiny would destroy their monopoly over the study of biological origins. It is simply not an option as far as they are concerned.

But digging in their heels and robotically maintaining the status quo is not a happy option either. Evolution has become totally status quo. Its supporters therefore tend to be stodgy and humorless (watch Ben Stein's *Expelled* and decide for yourself). They continually need to instruct the benighted masses why evolution shouldn't be criticized. Avoiding criticism by claiming to be beyond criticism seems hardly in the spirit of science.

We, on the other hand, can afford to keep our sense of humor. We don't have anything to lose. We don't have positions of authority to preserve. We don't have public moneys to administer. We don't have a professional guild that we need to keep happy for the sake of our careers. We can be free spirits. This sits especially well with young people, who thrive on rebelling against the status quo and don't enjoy having dogmatic Darwinists tell them what they must think and do.

Young people—people like you—are the scientists of tomorrow and the hope of intelligent design!

Op-Ed by Richard T. Halvorson

Does our culture, like many others, have an unpardonable heresy? Every culture constructs an idol unto itself, punishing heresy by excommunication. We can discover the sacred idol of any culture by finding its taboo question.

In Medieval Europe, the peasant was forbidden to question the truth of the Church. Under Communism, comrades doubting the Party were thrown in gulag labor camps. Now, citizens must recite principles of Darwinism through compulsory schooling.

We are encouraged to learn nuances like punctuated equilibrium and neo-Darwinism, but questioning the universal explanatory power of evolution is met with intellectual excommunication.

I make no apology for those who blindly reject scientific evidence due to contrived religious doctrines; I have equally little tolerance for those who ignore scientific evidence to prop up a naturalistic anti-religious dogma.

Anti-religious prejudice among scientists significantly impeded 20th century scientific advance. Stephen Hawking wrote in *A Brief History of Time* that evidence for the Big Bang was ignored for decades because it "smacks of divine intervention." For fear of theological implications, there were "a number of attempts to avoid the conclusion that there had been a Big Bang."

Intellectual honesty requires rationally examining our fundamental premises—yet expressing hesitation about Darwin is considered irretrievable intellectual suicide, the unthinkable doubt, the unpardonable sin of academia.

Although the postmodern era questions everything else—the possibility of knowledge, basic morality and reality itself—critical discussion of Darwin is taboo. While evolutionary biologists test Darwin's hypothesis in every experiment they conduct, the basic premise of evolution remains a scientific Holy of Holies, despite our absurd skepticism in other areas.

Oxford zoologist Richard Dawkins writes: "It is absolutely safe to say that, if you meet somebody who does not believe in evolution, that person is either ignorant, stupid, or insane."

Biologists continue to recite the worn credo, "the central, unifying principle of biology is the theory of evolution." But where would physics be if Einstein had been forced to chant, "the central, unifying principle of physics is Newtonian theory," until he could not see beyond its limitations?

Scientific innovations originate outside the dominant paradigm—demanding orthodoxy invites stagnation. Scientists who question evolution, like Intelligent Design theorists, do not reject evolution entirely, but argue that evidence supports a limited explanatory role. Faithful Darwinists, however, like Teilhard de Chardin, insist that evolution is "a general postulate to which all theories, all hypotheses, all systems must henceforth bow."

Luckily, no one needs a doctorate to separate honest skepticism from institutionalized dogma. Skip Evans, of the National Center for Science Education, worried that classroom discussions of evidence against evolution might "cast seeds of doubt in students' minds."

Professors expressing doubts about evolution are often ostracized, demoted or fired. A Baylor University professor found research funds rescinded because his project would undermine evolutionary presuppositions. Other skeptical professors have resorted to using pseudonyms, fearing for their jobs and careers if they openly publish contrary evidence.

Evolution skeptics are almost universally dismissed with an ad hominem charge of "religiously-motivated propaganda." Yet science students and professors consistently fail to address the merits of critics' arguments. They cannot answer the relevant evidential questions of: (1) what is the most compelling critique of evolution; (2) and on which points the evidence or arguments fail.

Most Darwinists have not read or considered biochemist Michael Behe, geneticist Michael Denton, embryologist Jonathan Wells, or information theorist William Dembski. These dissenting voices are systematically marginalized and silenced by academic McCarthyism.

We must refuse to bow to our culture's false idols. Science will not benefit from canonizing Darwin or making evolution an article of secular faith. We must reject intellectual excommunication as a valid form of dealing with criticism: the most important question for any society to ask is the one that is forbidden. [8]

Wolves in Sheep's Clothing

As you attempt to argue for intelligent design against Darwinian evolution, you'll discover a strange thing: Some of your most ardent opponents will be religious critics who claim that by accepting intelligent design you are actually denying the Christian faith. Come again? That's right, they'll claim that intelligent design is a religious heresy and that you need to renounce it before you can be a Christian. Your initial reaction to this charge may be to think these people are mad—after all, weren't all the great theologians of the past basically in favor of ID? But in fact, these religious critics of ID are quite sane, and it will help here to understand where they're coming from. Forewarned is forearmed.

We'll give only one example of how these wolves in sheep's clothing operate. Once you understand the pattern, you'll see how it works in other cases. We'll focus on Francisco Ayala, a former Catholic priest and one of the most prolific writers on evolution in America. In *Darwin's Gift to Science and Religion,* Ayala devotes some space to the science of ID but then focuses on his main target, the supposed incompatibility of ID with evil. Invariably, these religious critics argue that ID commits you to a non-Christian view of God's goodness—that's how to spot the wolf in sheep's clothing.

Thus, Ayala argues that any God who is also an intelligent designer makes the problem of evil insoluble because such a designer God would be responsible for all the botched and malevolent designs we see in nature. With Darwinian natural selection serving as a designer substitute, Ayala refers all those botched and malevolent designs to evolution (this, he thinks, gets God off the hook):

A major burden was removed from the shoulders of believers when convincing evidence was advanced that the design of organisms need not be attributed to the immediate agency of the Creator, but rather is an outcome of natural processes. If we claim that organisms and their parts have been specifically designed by God, we have to account for the incompetent design of the human jaw, the narrowness of the birth canal, and our poorly designed backbone, less than fittingly suited for walking upright. Proponents of ID would do well to acknowledge Darwin's revolution and accept natural selection as the process that accounts for the design of organisms, as well as for the dysfunctions, oddities, cruelties, and sadism that pervade the world of life. Attributing these to specific agency by the Creator amounts to blasphemy. Proponents and followers of ID are surely well-meaning people who do not intend such blasphemy, but this is how matters appear to a biologist concerned that God not be slandered with the imputation of incompetent design.[9]

For Ayala, the problem is that a designer God creates by direct intervention and thus must be held responsible for all the bad designs in the world. Ayala's proposed solution is therefore to have God set up a world in which natural selection brings about bad designs. But how does this address the underlying difficulty, which is that a creator God has set up the conditions under which bad designs emerge? In the one case, this God acts directly; in the other, indirectly. But a creator God, as the source of all being, is as responsible in the one case as in the other. What difference does it make if a mugger brutalizes someone with his own hands (by direct means) or employs a vicious dog on a leash (by indirect means) to do the same? The mugger is equally guilty in both cases.

The same holds for a creator God who creates by direct intervention or by harnessing ordinary causes (compare God directly raising

Christ from the dead with God sending a wind to part the Red Sea). That's why so much of contemporary theology has a problem not just with ID but also with the traditional doctrine of creation that makes God the source of all being. The rage these days in theology is to shrink the power of God so that God is held in check by the world and thus cannot be held responsible for the world's evil. But this is not a Christian option. Accordingly, religious believers who hold to a traditional doctrine of creation and accept natural selection as God's method of creating organisms confront the problem of evil with the same force as believers with the same doctrine of God who reject natural selection and accept ID.

By the way, how do Christians make sense of the problem of evil in creation? Christianity holds that all evil in the world ultimately traces back to human sin. The *Catholic Encyclopedia* makes precisely this point:

> Christian philosophy has, like the Hebrew, uniformly attributed moral and physical evil to the action of created free will. Man has himself brought about the evil from which he suffers by transgressing the law of God, on obedience to which his happiness depended...The errors of mankind, mistaking the true conditions of its own well-being, have been the cause of moral and physical evil.[10]

For an account of what this means and how it can be, look for my (Bill's) forthcoming book *The End of Christianity: Finding a Good God in an Evil World*.

Making a Difference

Given the importance of this debate, you may wonder, "What can I do about it?" Here are a few things you can do to make a difference for the design revolution:[11]

Inform yourself. All of us, whether in class or in personal interactions, will have discussions about evolution and design. If you don't know what the issues are and haven't reflected on them, you can't take the first step. This book is a great start, but you'll need to dig deeper. You'll find the resources in appendix A tremendously useful. Read especially *The Design of Life* (by Bill and his colleague Jonathan Wells) to understand the nitty-gritty of ID and *Total Truth* (by Nancy Pearcey) to understand how ID fits in the larger cultural conversation.

Ask the right questions. Phillip Johnson's latest book is titled *The Right Questions.* Asking the right questions helps us to grasp an issue with clarity, to gather information, to illustrate weaknesses in an opposing position, and to shift the burden of proof when necessary. By asking the right questions about Darwinism, you throw the spotlight on problem areas that Darwinists try to cover up.

Appeal to the undecided middle. Hard-core critics of ID are unlikely to be won over to ID, at least not immediately. But in your conversations and debates with hard-core critics, often people from the undecided middle are watching. Make your case to them. You'll be surprised how many are favorably impressed with ID once they understand how much more it has going for it than the hard-core critics pretend. (See appendix D.)

Use this book as a resource. Teach a class on ID using *Understanding Intelligent Design* at a church or local community center. Lead a small group (for example, a church fellowship group) based on this book. Give a copy to a teacher, youth pastor, or skeptical friend, and ask for honest feedback.

Get active online. The Internet is a wild place, but it is a great place to toss around ideas, get feedback, and influence people. It's also a place to sharpen your debating skills. You can start a blog or join an existing blog (see the URLs for Bill's and Sean's blogs in appendix A). Online communities and chat groups are also available. But be careful. It would be good to accompany a seasoned veteran as you enter the world of Internet Darwinists—a more vicious bunch is hard to imagine.

Write to your local paper. Your local newspaper will carry letters and longer opinion pieces, known as op-eds, that can have a considerable impact on the thinking of your community. As issues arise locally concerning ID, write your local newspaper a letter or op-ed defending it. The op-ed by Richard Halvorson reprinted earlier in this chapter provides a shining example of what we have in mind.

Form a local pro-ID group. This can be a reading group, in which you systematically go through the ID literature. It can take a more activist role, such as starting a petition to support the objective teaching of Darwinian evolution so that the evidence that both confirms and disconfirms it gets taught. Your group may be affiliated with a larger organizing body. If, for instance, you are on a college or high school campus, you can form an IDEA club (Intelligent Design and Evolution Awareness). To start such a club, visit www.ideacenter.org/clubs.

Organize local pro-ID events. For instance, sponsor an ID speaker at a local school, community center, or church. We both speak regularly to a variety of audiences on the topic of design. Alternatively, arrange to show a video on ID. *Unlocking the Mystery of Life* (see appendix A) is a must-see for anyone interested in intelligent design.

Give money and time. Pro-ID organizations need your financial help. These are nonprofit organizations whose survival depends on the donations of private individuals and groups. Darwinists often make off that ID is incredibly well funded by right-wing extremists intent on taking over the United States. The reality is quite different. The design community operates on a shoestring. Funding and university appointments (which are often paid for by your tax dollars) are regularly withheld from ID proponents, so ID's financial support depends on you. But money isn't the only thing you can give. Giving of your time is also extremely important. What if biology textbooks in your state blatantly misrepresent the actual strength of Darwin's theory. Will you be there at the textbook hearings to voice your concerns?

Get a Ph.D. It usually takes ten years from the time you get your high school diploma till you get a Ph.D.—if, that is, you stay in school right through. Delay your gratification of getting a high-paying job right now; stay a student and take your rewards down the line. Ten years gets you to the place where you can become an active researcher contributing to the advance of ID! Too many people are on the sidelines cheering for ID. ID has lots of sympathizers, but it has a critical shortage of trained professionals who can do the heavy lifting. Will you become one?

Joining the Revolution

As we conclude, we have a final challenge for you. Since you have made it this far through the book (unless you just skipped to the end to see how it finishes), you most likely are convinced that ID is important. You understand what is at stake. You realize that the debate over ID is not just about science. It has profound implications for all aspects of life.

So here is the challenge: Will you be a part of the design revolution? Will you enter the discussion? Will you be a difference maker and take at least some of the steps outlined in the last section? As critical as this revolution is, its outcome is not guaranteed. It will only succeed if many people—many *young* people—rise up and take action. The future depends on you. Be a hero.

Appendix A

Recommended Resources

Websites

www.designinference.com (Bill's personal website)

www.uncommondescent.com (Bill's blog)

www.seanmcdowell.org (Sean's personal website)

www.intelligentdesign.org (portal site)

www.idthefuture.com (podcasts)

www.discovery.org/csc (ID's main think tank)

www.evolutionnews.org (critiquing evolution)

www.intelligentdesignnetwork.org (getting ID into schools)

www.exploreevolution.org (getting evolution taught fairly)

www.ideacenter.org (campus student chapters focusing on ID)

www.overwhelmingevidence.com (community site for high school students)

www.dissentfromdarwin.org (scientists who dissent from Darwin)

www.discovery.org/a/2640 (peer-reviewed articles supporting ID)

www.biologicinstitute.org (research lab devoted to ID)

www.EvoInfo.org (research lab exploring limits of evolution)

www.arn.org (ID books, paraphernalia, and discussion)

www.probe.org (apologetics and ID)

Books

Beauregard, Mario, and Denyse O'Leary. *The Spiritual Brain*. New York: HarperOne, 2007. Shows how ID extends to the mind-body problem of neuroscience.

Behe, Michael. *Darwin's Black Box*. New York: Free Press, 1996. Groundbreaking work that outlined a positive ID alternative to Darwinism.

Dembski, William A., ed. *Uncommon Dissent: Intellectuals Who Find Darwinism Unconvincing*. Wilmington, DE: ISI Books, 2004. Shows that not all the smart people are Darwinists.

Dembski, William A., and Jonathan Wells. *The Design of Life*. Dallas: Foundation for Thought and Ethics, 2008. Best in-depth treatment of design in biology.

Flew, Antony, with Roy Abraham Varghese. *There Is a God: How the World's Most Notorious Atheist Changed His Mind*. New York: HarperOne, 2007. Treats ID's crucial role in Flew's deconversion from atheism.

Gonzalez, Guillermo, and Jay W. Richards. *The Privileged Planet*. Washington, DC: Regnery, 2004. Best in-depth treatment of design in cosmology.

Johnson, Phillip E. *Darwin on Trial*, 2nd ed. Downers Grove, IL: InterVarsity, 1993. Classic critique of Darwinism that propelled the ID movement. Originally published 1991.

Newman, Robert C., and John L. Wiester. *What's Darwin Got to Do with It?* Downers Grove, IL: InterVarsity, 2000. Cartoon book for junior high students discussing Darwinism and design.

Pearcey, Nancy. *Total Truth: Liberating Christianity from Its Cultural Captivity*. Wheaton, IL: Crossway, 2004. Situates ID within the broader cultural conversation.

Wells, Jonathan. *Icons of Evolution*. Washington, DC: Regnery, 2000. Debunks the main textbook evidences for Darwinism.

Wiker, Benjamin. *Moral Darwinism*. Downers Grove, IL: Inter-Varsity, 2002. Traces the philosophical roots of Darwinian naturalism from ancient to modern times.

Woodward, Thomas. *Doubts about Darwin: A History of Intelligent Design*. Grand Rapids: Baker, 2003. Best early history of ID movement.

DVDs

The Case for a Creator (www.illustramedia.com)

Expelled: No Intelligence Allowed (www.expelledthemovie.com)

Icons of Evolution (www.coldwatermedia.com)

The Privileged Planet (www.illustramedia.com)

Redeeming Darwin: Discovering the Designer (www.probe.org)

Unlocking the Mystery of Life (www.illustramedia.com)

Appendix B

Quick Response Guide

To engage effectively in discussions about ID, you need to be prepared to answer the most common objections. Although we have dealt with these at greater length throughout this book, we want to list quick responses to those objections you are most likely to encounter in conversations about design.

OBJECTION 1: ID makes no predictions.

RESPONSE: ID predicts that there should be structures beyond the reach of chance-based Darwinian mechanisms. And there are (for example, the bacterial flagellum).

OBJECTION 2: ID is religiously motivated.

RESPONSE: ID constructs a scientific case against Darwinian evolution. The motivation of its advocates is irrelevant. Stephen Hawking hopes his work in physics will help us understand the mind of God. Steven Weinberg hopes his work in physics will help to destroy religion. Do their motivations invalidate their science? Of course not.

OBJECTION 3: ID argues from ignorance.

RESPONSE: ID not only identifies holes in Darwinian evolution but also explores positive features of design present in biological systems, such as the specified complexity in DNA and the molecular machinery inside cells.

OBJECTION 4: ID violates the scientific consensus.

RESPONSE: So did Copernicus, Galileo, Kepler, Newton, and even Darwin himself! The point of science is not to protect a consensus but to provide an accurate understanding of the universe, and that requires a readiness to break with consensus.

OBJECTION 5: ID is a science stopper.

RESPONSE: ID encourages science in ways that Darwinism hinders. Darwinism, for example, predicts that a lot of DNA is junk. Intelligent design encourages the ongoing search for function in DNA. In this regard, ID has been vindicated over Darwinism. ID keeps Darwinism honest. It therefore can't be a science stopper.

OBJECTION 6: ID violates the scientific method.

RESPONSE: The scientific method tests hypotheses in light of evidence. ID does this too. For example, it tests the hypothesis that irreducibly complex systems are designed by gauging the power of Darwinian evolutionary mechanisms to produce them.

OBJECTION 7: Imperfection in living things counts against design.

RESPONSE: Imperfection speaks to the quality of design, not to its reality. No one seriously thinks that design must be perfect to be detectable. Because ecological balance demands that all life forms must die and be recycled, some imperfection is unavoidable.

OBJECTION 8: ID is Bible-based.

RESPONSE: While the findings of ID are consistent with the Bible, the evidence for design comes from cosmology, physics, chemistry, biology, information theory, and other scientific disciplines.

OBJECTION 9: No peer-reviewed journal articles supporting ID exist.

RESPONSE: Although articles supporting ID have difficulty gaining a fair hearing, a growing number of peer-reviewed journal articles and books supporting design do in fact exist (see www.discovery.org/a/2640).

Objection 10: No credible scholars support ID.

Response: University of Georgia professor Henry Schaefer III, one of the most widely cited chemists in the world with more than 1000 publications, supports ID. So do other prominent scientists at places like Princeton, USC, and Baylor. Many more would publicly embrace ID but for the persecution they would encounter from Darwinists (see Ben Stein's documentary *Expelled: No Intelligence Allowed*).

Appendix C

Ten Questions to Ask Your Science Teacher About Design

1. Design Detection

If nature, or some aspect of it, were intelligently designed, how could we tell?

Design inferences in the past were largely informal and intuitive. Usually people knew it when they saw it. Intelligent design, by introducing specified complexity, makes the detection of design rigorous. Something is complex if it is hard to reproduce by chance and specified if it matches an independently given pattern (such as the faces on Mt. Rushmore). Specified complexity gives a precise criterion for reliably inferring intelligence (see chapter 6).

2. Looking for Design in Biology

Should biologists be encouraged to look for signs of intelligence in biological systems? Why or why not?

Scientists today look for signs of intelligence in many places, including distant space (consider SETI, the search for extraterrestrial intelligence). Yet many biologists regard as illegitimate the search for signs of intelligence in biological systems. Why arbitrarily exclude design inferences from biology if we accept them for other scientific disciplines (see chapter 5)? The reality of the apparent design in nature is an open question.

3. The Rules of Science

Who determines the rules of science? Are these rules written in stone? Is it mandatory that scientific explanations only appeal to matter and energy operating by unbroken natural laws (a principle known as methodological naturalism)?

The rules of science are not written in stone. They have been negotiated over many centuries as science (formerly called "natural philosophy") has tried to understand the natural world. These rules have changed in the past, and they will change in the future. Right now much of the scientific community is bewitched by a view of science called methodological naturalism, which says that science may only offer naturalistic explanations. But science seeks to understand nature. If intelligent causes operate in nature, methodological naturalism must not be used to rule them out.

4. Biology's Information Problem

How do we account for the complex information-rich patterns in biological systems? What is the source of that information?

The central problem for biology is information (see chapter 7). Living things are not mere lumps of matter. Life is special, and what makes life special is the arrangement of its matter into very specific *forms*. In other words, what makes life special is in*form*ation. Where did the information necessary for life come from? Where did the information necessary for the Cambrian explosion come from (see chapter 4)? How can a blind material process generate the novel information of biological systems? ID argues that such information has an intelligent source.

5. Molecular Machines

Do any structures in the cell resemble machines designed by humans? How do we account for such structures?

The biological world is full of molecular machines that are strikingly similar to humanly made machines (see chapters 7 and 8). In fact, they are more than similar. Just about every engineering principle that we employ in our own machines gets used at the molecular level, with this exception: The technology inside the cell vastly exceeds human technology. How then do biologists explain the origin of such structures? How can a blind material process generate the multiple coordinated changes needed to build a molecular machine? If we see a level of engineering inside the cell that far surpasses our own abilities, we can reasonably conclude that these molecular machines are actually, and not merely apparently, designed.

6. Irreducible Complexity

What are irreducibly complex systems? Do such systems exist in biology? If so, are those systems evidence for design? If not, why not?

The biological world is full of functioning molecular systems that cannot be simplified without losing the system's function (see chapter 8). Take away parts, and the system's function cannot be recovered. Such systems are called irreducibly complex. How do evolutionary theorists propose to account for such systems? What detailed, testable, step-by-step proposals explain the emergence of irreducibly complex machines such as the flagellum? Given that intelligence is known to design such systems, it is a reasonable inference to conclude that they were designed.

7. Similar Structures

Human designers reuse designs that work well. Life forms also reuse certain structures (the camera eye, for example, appears in humans and octopuses). How well does this evidence support Darwinian evolution? Does it support intelligent design more strongly?

Evolutionary biologists attribute similar biological structures to either common descent or convergence. Structures are said to result from convergence if they evolved independently from distinct lines of organisms. Darwinian explanations of convergence strain credulity because they must account for how trial-and-error tinkering (natural selection acting on random variations) could produce strikingly similar structures in widely different organisms and environments. It's one thing for evolution to explain similarity by common descent—the same structure is then just carried along in different lineages. It's another to explain it as the result of blind tinkering that happened to hit on the same structure multiple times. Design proponents attribute such similar structures to common design (just as an engineer may use the same parts in different machines). If human designers frequently reuse successful designs, the designer of nature can surely do the same.

8. Fine-Tuning

The laws of physics are fine-tuned to allow life to exist. Since designers are capable of fine-tuning a system, can design be considered the best explanation for the universe?

Physicists agree that the constants of nature have a strange thing in common: They seem precisely calibrated for the existence of life (see chapter 9). As Frederick Hoyle famously remarked, it appears that someone has "monkeyed" with physics. Naturalistic explanations that attempt to account for this eerie fine-tuning invariably introduce entities for which there is no independent evidence (for example, they invoke multiple worlds with which we have no physical way of interacting). The fine-tuning of the universe strongly suggests that it was intelligently designed.

9. The Privileged Planet

The earth seems ideally positioned in our galaxy for complex life to exist and for scientific discovery to advance. Does this privileged status of earth indicate intelligent design? Why or why not?

Many factors had to come together on earth for human life to exist (chapter 9). We exist in just the right place in just the right type of galaxy at just the right cosmic moment. We orbit the right type of star at the right distance for life. The earth has large surrounding planets to protect us from comets, a moon to direct important life-permitting cycles, and an iron core that protects us from harmful radiation. Moreover, the earth has many features that facilitate scientific discovery, such as a moon that makes possible perfect eclipses. Humans seem ideally situated on the earth to make scientific discoveries. This suggests that a designer designed our place in the world so that we can understand the world's design. Naturalism, by contrast, leaves it a complete mystery why we should be able to do science and gain insight into the underlying structure of the world.

10. The Origin of the Universe

The universe gives every indication of having a beginning. Since something cannot come from nothing, is it legitimate to conclude that a designer made the universe? If not, why not?

For most of world history, scientists believed the universe was eternal. With advances in our understanding of cosmology over the past 40 years, however, scientists now recognize that the universe had a beginning and is finite in duration and size. In other words, the universe has not always been there. Since the universe had a beginning, why not conclude that it had a designer that brought it into existence? Since matter, space, and time themselves had a beginning, this would suggest that the universe had a non-physical, non-spatial, and non-temporal cause. A designer in the mold of the Christian God certainly fits the bill.

Appendix D

Dealing with
Difficult Critics of ID

Many critics of ID think that intelligent design is so utterly mistaken that there's no debate worth having—the only appropriate action is to destroy it! As a consequence, they engage in all forms of character assassination, ad hominem attacks, guilt by association, and demonization. My (Bill's) favorite example is Marshal Berman's article in the *American Biology Teacher* (December 2003) titled "Intelligent Design Creationism: A Threat to Society—Not Just Biology." It starts with the famous quote from Edmund Burke: "The only thing necessary for the triumph of evil is for good men to do nothing." For Berman, intelligent design is not just mistaken but evil.

Usually the attacks are more subtle. Imagine if someone critical of Darwinian evolution decided to publish a book titled *Dogmatic Darwinian Fundamentalists and Their Critics,* got permission to republish articles by prominent Darwinists without their knowledge, and then put their articles in a collection of critical replies designed to make them look foolish. Evolutionists would howl.

A few years ago, Robert Pennock published a collection of essays titled *Intelligent Design Creationism and Its Critics.* When the book appeared, I (Bill) was surprised to learn that I had two essays in it. Without my knowledge, Pennock had approached the publishers of those two essays and gotten their permission to reprint them. It seemed to the average reader that I had given my permission to have the essays appear in a book identifying (dismissing) my position as a form of creationism and subjecting my essays to criticism I had no chance to refute. I would never have given my permission with that title—but no one asked me.

Sometimes the attacks obscure basic issues. Michael Behe and I (Bill) debated Pennock and Kenneth Miller at the American Museum of Natural History in the spring of 2002. The debate was initially titled "Blind Evolution or Intelligent Design?" Yet when the debate actually took place, the organizers had quietly dropped the word *blind* from the program bulletin and retitled the debate simply "Evolution or Intelligent Design?"

The original title was more accurate. Intelligent design is opposed to blind evolution, not to evolution guided by a designing intelligence—that would be a form of intelligent design. By *evolution,* our critics mean a blind form of it—that is, a form of evolution occurring entirely by undirected material mechanisms. But calling attention to the blindness, or absence of design, in the evolutionary process is clearly not in their interest.

For now, the evolutionists are sitting pretty. They hold the reins of power in the academy, they control federal research funds, and they have unlimited access to the media. Intelligent design has become such a threat to them because it gives the majority of Americans, who do not buy the atheistic picture of evolution peddled in all the textbooks, the tools with which to effectively challenge the evolutionists' power. As a result, the evolutionists have adopted a zero-concession policy toward intelligent design. Absolutely nothing is to be conceded to intelligent design and its proponents. To hope for concessions is therefore futile.

Engaging the Hard Core

Hard-core critics who have adopted this policy are still worth engaging, but we need to control the terms of engagement. When engaging them, the furthest thing from our minds should be to convert them, to win them over, to appeal to their good will, to make our cause seem reasonable in their eyes. Yes, with God all things are possible. But we need to set wishful thinking firmly to one side.

The point is not to change our critics' minds, but instead to clarify our arguments, to address weaknesses in our own position, to identify areas requiring further work and study, and perhaps most significantly, to appeal to the undecided middle that is watching this debate and trying to sort through the issues. The proper answer to the critics' zero-concession policy is therefore a "there might be something to it after all" policy.

Think of attacks by our critics as opportunities to advance ID. The Israelite conquest of the promised land is our model: The Israelites would approach a fortified city. Their inhabitants, instead of entrenching themselves and allowing their countryside to be ravaged, would then come out for battle. Once they left their positions of safety, the Israelites would make short work of them.

That is the pattern in the debate over ID. The proponents of evolution prefer to stay in their fortified positions. They do not want to dignify us by devoting time and energy to refute us. They prefer to ignore us. They wish we would just go away. But the challenge to evolutionary dogma in the schools and public square is real and threatens their monopoly. The unwashed masses are not with them. The evolutionists cannot leave these crazy design theorists unanswered. So out they come from their positions of safety to challenge us. But in the very challenge, they open evolutionary theory to a scrutiny it cannot withstand (see the ten questions in appendix C).

To understand how to defend ourselves in this debate, we need first to understand the forms that the attacks take. The attacks take three forms, corresponding to the three traditional appeals of rhetoric: logos, ethos, and pathos. Logos refers to the reasoned case that is being advanced. Think of it as the formal argument that can be written out on a sheet of paper. The identification of presuppositions, the marshalling of evidence, and the drawing of inferences all fall under logos. Ethos refers to the perceived character, integrity, and accomplishment of the speaker and his subject. It inspires confidence and establishes credibility in the eyes of the audience or destroys confidence and erodes credibility. And finally, pathos refers to the emotion or passion that the speaker is able to elicit from the audience. Is the speaker able to play on the audience's heartstrings and elicit sympathy or perhaps inspire anger or fear? Pathos is especially important if one is trying to get the audience to take action.

Evolutionists use each of these to attack intelligent design. They attack ID with respect to logos by claiming that science utterly fails to support it, whether on evidential or theoretical grounds. They attack it with respect to ethos by charging its proponents with being everything from immoral to stupid. And finally, they attack it with respect to pathos by instilling the fear that intelligent design means not just the end of science but the end of rational discourse in a free and open society. Let us look at these attacks more closely and especially at ways to counter them.

Staying on Topic

Usually, in keeping with the no-concession policy, an attack against ID relating to logos starts with some blanket dismissal, such as "Intelligent design offers no testable hypotheses," or "Intelligent design is just an argument from ignorance," or "Intelligent design is incoherent because of the poor design evident in biological systems." To counter these attacks, we have to stay on topic. The question that must always be kept front and center in addressing ID's critics is this: Why should material mechanisms always trump intelligent design in explaining the complexity and diversity of living forms?

The naturalistic scientist resists this question (and this includes religious believers who think that science must understand nature entirely in terms of material processes that give no evidence of design). Indeed, from a naturalistic vantage point, what else could be responsible for life's complexity and diversity except unguided material mechanisms?

The naturalist sees designing engineers as appearing only after evolution—a naturalistic form of it—has run its course. That's why Daniel Hillis remarks, "There are only two ways we know of to make extremely complicated things, one is by engineering, and the other is evolution. And of the two, evolution will make the more complex."

But whether a purely materialistic form of evolution can perform amazing feats of design that would otherwise require super-engineers is precisely the point at issue. Unless we press this point, evolutionists win by default, having defined science as the study of material processes that, by logical necessity, disqualify design and ensure that some materialistic account of evolution must be true.

Peripheral Issues

Attacks against intelligent design based on ethos focus on peripheral issues, such as whether design theorists have published their ideas in the right places, whether the scientific community is accepting intelligent design in sufficient numbers to render it credible, whether intelligent design is being unduly politicized, whether design theorists are religiously motivated, and so on. Such questions are interesting, but they do not address the validity of intelligent design as an intellectual and scientific project, nor do they assess its truth or falsehood. Nonetheless, such questions are important to people on the sidelines. We therefore need to make certain that we are not misrepresented here.

Take the question of peer review. Intelligent design is a minority position only now beginning to gain a hearing in the mainstream, peer-reviewed literature, but our critics contend that it has no presence in that literature whatsoever. For instance, Eugenie Scott at the National Center for Science Education claimed that my (Bill's) book *The Design Inference* was not peer-reviewed. But it had appeared as part of a Cambridge University Press monograph series (Cambridge Studies in Probability, Induction, and Decision Theory) with an academic editorial board that included members of the National Academy of Sciences as well as one Nobel laureate, and the manuscript had to be passed by three anonymous expert referees before Cambridge University Press would publish it.

Similarly, at the *Design and Its Critics* conference (held at

Concordia University in the summer of 2000), Kenneth Miller claimed that Michael Behe's notion of irreducible complexity was nowhere to be found in the mainstream, peer-reviewed biological literature. Yet in fact, two mainstream scientists had just a few months earlier published an article in the *Journal of Theoretical Biology* on that very topic.

We do not need to respond to every misrepresentation that the other side makes. It is enough to respond to those that trouble the undecided middle. And even here, let us be careful not to become defensive. In line with our "there might be something to it after all" policy, it is usually enough to indicate that there is more to the story than the other side lets on. Rhetorician John Angus Campbell, a good friend of the ID movement, puts it this way: A draw is a win.

The other side wants to obliterate intelligent design. Yet to persuade the undecided middle, we just have to show that intelligent design has something going for it. As much as possible, therefore, let us always return to the main point at issue, which is that unguided material mechanisms lack the creative capacity to bring about the complexity and diversity of living forms and that the ID movement is helping to clarify this central issue in biology.

What Counts as Evidence?

How do we determine whether certain data count as evidence supporting a hypothesis? This question may strike us as uncontroversial. But in fact, it can be highly controversial. What it means for something to count as evidence is not itself decided by evidence. Rather, it depends on certain predispositions, and these are heavily influenced by our worldview.

For the materialist, no facts of biology could count as evidence for intelligent design because no designer exists—which is a philosophical, not a scientific, assumption. Thus, when materialists claim that no evidence supports intelligent design, it is appropriate to ask whether any data from biology could even in principle provide such evidence, and if so, what these data might look like. If the answer is that no data could even in principle provide support for intelligent design, the conversation has moved from science to philosophy.

In science, no raw data exist. Data are always collected in light of background knowledge and assumptions. These influence the aspects of nature to which we attend and how we collect our data. Once we have collected the data, we interpret them. At one level of interpretation, we see facts. At a higher level of interpretation, we see patterns connecting these facts. At still higher levels of interpretation, we formulate hypotheses and theories to make sense of these patterns. It follows that, as an interpretive enterprise, science can never guarantee consensus, especially at the higher levels of interpretation.

More and more, critics of intelligent design are outraged by what they call *quote mining*. They fault design theorists for going to the biological literature to pull out quotes and ideas that support intelligent design. The critics are outraged because they see the design theorists as shamelessly exploiting the hard scientific work of others and interpreting it in ways that the scientists who originally did the work would reject. We have nothing to be ashamed of here. As Nobel laureate William Lawrence Bragg remarked, "The important thing in science is not so much to obtain new facts as to discover new ways of thinking about them." Intelligent design is doing just that—discovering new ways of thinking about and interpreting the well-established facts of science that pertain to biological complexity and diversity.

Fear, Loathing, and Labeling

Finally, let us turn to attacks against intelligent design that appeal to pathos. The strategy of the other side here is clear: induce (in the undecided middle) fear and loathing of intelligent design—fear that science and society will be subverted, and loathing that intelligent design is just a tool for advancing religious and political extremism. By contrast, to promote intelligent design with regard to pathos, the most effective approach is to appeal to the undecided middle's sense of fair play, especially its tendency to root for the underdog and for freedom of expression.

In practice, to induce fear and loathing of intelligent design, the other side invokes pejorative labels that are rich in negative associations. *Creationism* is by far the preferred pejorative, though *antievolution, antiscience, fundamentalism, right-wing extremism,* and *pseudoscience* are great favorites as well. As far as possible, we need to resist being labeled. To do this effectively, however, simply denying a label is not enough. In fact, being too vocal and adamant about denying a label can be a good way of attaching it more firmly.

Denial works best if we are explicitly asked to comment on a label and then can explain why the label is wrong or misleading. Most reporters who interview me (Bill) ask how intelligent design differs from creationism. That gives me a perfect opening, and I can explain how intelligent design is not a religious doctrine about where everything came from but rather a scientific investigation into how patterns in nature can signify intelligence. If the reporters assume that the two are the same, I take the chance to explain the difference.

The best way to resist being labeled, however, is not by denying the labels but by developing our own vocabulary and ideas that set the agenda for the debate over biological origins. In this way, the other side is increasingly forced to engage our ideas on our terms and cannot rely on dismissive labels to avoid intellectual work. Consider the following terms: *irreducible complexity, specified complexity, design inference, explanatory filter,* and *empirical detectability of design.* The other side now spends an enormous amount of time discussing these terms and the ideas underlying them. Insofar as the other side engages us on our terms, it is in no position to label us.

Of course, the other side sees this and therefore tries to make its labels stick. Still, we do ourselves good by steering the discussion as much as possible to matters of substance and avoiding labels. Clarity and consistency in how we express our ideas are the best antidotes to labeling by the other side. Increasingly, the media are now grasping our ideas and expressing them not with tendentious labels but in our own words. For instance, the media now consistently refer to intelligent design and not to creationism or intelligent-design creationism.

Not all labels, however, have the intended negative effect. There is no way to give the labels *antiscience* or *pseudoscience* a positive spin, but what about *antievolution*? The evolutionists who are our main critics think evolution is the greatest concept ever conceived. In *Darwin's Dangerous Idea*, Daniel Dennett remarked: "If I were to give an award for the single best idea anyone has ever had, I'd give it to Darwin, ahead of Newton and Einstein and everyone else. In a single stroke, the idea of evolution by natural selection unifies the realm of life, meaning, and purpose with the realm of space and time, cause and effect, mechanism and physical law."

For most of the population, however, the term *evolution* holds no such positive associations. For most people, evolution is an implausible and controversy-ridden theory of biological origins, one that gives comfort to atheists and undermines religious faith. When our opponents describe intelligent design as a form of antievolutionism, they give it a positive advertisement in some circles.

Even so, there is an important clarification to keep in mind here. Intelligent design is antievolution not in the sense of rejecting all evolutionary change. Indeed, some design theorists, like Michael Behe, accept a lot of evolutionary change. Rather, intelligent design is antievolution in the limited sense that it regards blind material forces as inadequate for explaining all evolutionary change.

Maintaining Composure

We can resist intimidation and maintain our composure in the face of evolutionist opposition. To do this, two extremes must be avoided. On the one hand, we must refuse to allow evolutionists to send us cowering into a corner. This depends on doing our homework so that we know what we are talking about, and on going out and mixing it up with enough evolutionists so that we know what we are up against.

On the other hand, we must refuse to allow evolutionists to make us angry and lose our self-control, which usually leads us to denounce our opponents in harsh and bitter words, and these never help our cause. Aggressiveness and argumentativeness are almost always interpreted as defensiveness, and rightly so. Victor Hugo put it this way: "Strong and bitter words indicate a weak cause."

I (Bill) do a fair amount of public speaking and know from experience how it feels when a questioner gets under my skin and I'm tempted to let him have it. The simplest way I've found to resist that urge is simply to stay on topic, to answer the questioner's actual questions, to be courteous throughout, and as much as possible, to attribute to the questioner sincere motives. This has several advantages: It prevents you from seeming defensive; it wins the respect of the audience (and they're the ones we're trying to reach); and it is usually the best way to slap some sense into an unruly questioner, whose aim is to distract you from your message. By refusing to be distracted, you reinforce your message.

Evolutionists often radiate confidence—as though their theory is the cat's meow and they've got everything sewed up. Design advocates, notwithstanding, are in a much better position to radiate confidence. Here's why. The evolutionists are essentially fighting a defensive war. If they could demonstrate the power of material mechanisms to generate biological complexity and diversity, we would not be having this debate. Phillip Johnson's *Darwin on Trial* would never have been written, and the intelligent design movement would not exist. Evolutionists profess that they have the greatest scientific theory ever put forward. In fact, their emperor has no clothes!*

---

* This appendix is adapted from Bill's essay "Winning by Design" in *Touchstone* (July/August 2004). The essay is available online at touchstonemag.com/archives/article.php?id=17-06-054-f.

Appendix E

Evolutionary Logic:
A Parody of Darwinian
Educational Philosophy

With the rise of neo-Darwinism in the 1930s, evolutionary biology became a growth industry. That growth has resulted in the demand for more flexible methods of establishing evolutionary biology's grandiose claims than the laborious, difficult, pedantic, and rigorous methods favored throughout the rest of the sciences. This demand has been met by what is now a well-developed branch of evolutionary biology known as *evolutionary logic*.

We can't here develop the theory of evolutionary logic in detail, but we can introduce some necessary terminology. In ordinary logic, which is used throughout the rest of the sciences, one is justified asserting that a claim is true provided one can construct a coherent and rigorous argument to support it. In evolutionary logic we relax both these restrictions: An evolutionary claim is true provided there is an evolutionary argument that supports it. This definition is sufficiently clear as not to require elaboration. Further, we stipulate that any circularity in this definition is virtuous rather than vicious.

The benefits and practical applications of evolutionary logic will be obvious. Professional authors of evolutionary tracts depend on it for their livelihood. Instructors in evolutionary biology find that evolutionary logic enables them to make complex ideas readily accessible to students regardless of their preparation or background. Indeed, proficiency in evolutionary logic has been shown to be positively correlated with high self-esteem.

Research workers in a hurry to claim priority for a new result or who lack the time and inclination for genuine scholarship find evolutionary logic useful for expeditiously writing up their results. In this respect, evolutionary logic has a further advantage, namely, the results are not required to be true, thus eliminating a wearisome (and now unnecessary) restriction on the growth of evolutionary knowledge.

Let us next consider some of the actual techniques for establishing evolutionary claims that evolutionary logic makes available. We will focus mainly on ways in which these techniques can be applied in lecture courses—they require only trivial modification to be used in textbooks, research papers, formal debates, and Internet discussions.

In evolutionary biology, organisms change by an evolutionary process into other organisms. This means that evolutionary biologists are often called on to establish lineal relationships. There is a whole class of methods that can be applied when an instructor can't quite bridge an evolutionary gap.

Suppose an instructor can get from organism A to organism B and from organism C to organism D by an evolutionary process but can't bridge the gap between B and C. A number of techniques are available to the aggressive instructor in this emergency. The instructor can write down B and then, without any hesitation, put "therefore C." If the class is bored or the organisms in question are not terribly interesting, it is unlikely that anyone will question the "therefore." This is the method of *argument by omission,* and it is remarkably easy to foist on unwary students.

In the *argument by fiat,* one merely conjectures an intermediary between B and C—call it Z—that shares characteristics of both. The evolutionary transitions from B to Z and then from Z to C are now obvious. Of course, Z only exists in one's imagination and not in the real world. (This is not a problem. Evolutionary theory admits no hard-and-fast distinction between the imaginary and the real.)

The argument by fiat is a special case of the *argument by misdirection,* where in place of a difficult problem that was supposed to be solved, one solves an easier problem that is superficially similar to the original problem.

Argument by definition is devilishly clever. Here the instructor defines a set S to be whatever biological systems satisfy some property. For instance, S might consist of all irreducibly complex molecular machines that are the result of Darwinian evolution. The lecturer then announces that in the future only members of S will be the focus of discussion. Even honors students will fall into this trap, not questioning whether the set S might in fact be empty.

To shut down discussion, nothing beats a*rgument by assertion.* If, for instance, some vague waffle about an evolutionary transition does not satisfy an unruly student, the instructor simply says, "This point should be intuitively obvious. I've explained it as clearly as I can. If you still cannot see it, you will just have to think very carefully about it yourself, and then you will see how trivial and obvious it is."

The instructor at this point might also want to add, "What are you, a creationist?" or "Are you one of those Christian fundamentalists?" *Arguments by demonization* like this are particularly effective when one or a few students get unruly but the majority sides with the instructor.

When the majority of the class becomes unruly, the technique of choice is *argument by obscure reference.* This will silence all but the most resolute troublemaker. Few students take the time to hunt down an obscure reference in the evolutionary literature. And even if students locate the reference (which is becoming easier with the Internet), if the reference is sufficiently technical and difficult to understand, the instructor can easily inform the student that he or she simply doesn't understand the relevant passage.

In this case, if the instructor is feeling generous, he or she may simply offer an *argument from removable ignorance*—"Just keep studying evolutionary theory, and eventually it will all make sense." If that doesn't work, the instructor may wish to try an *argument from stupidity*—"How can you be so stupid?" But if the student is otherwise at the top of the class, this approach may backfire. In that case, either the *argument from wickedness* ("You are just being perverse") or the *argument from insanity* ("What are you, nuts?" or "Have you been brainwashed?") should do the trick. And always keep the *argument by demonization* in your front pocket.

A variant of the argument by obscure reference is the *argument by irrelevant reference*. This works in a pinch when you can be reasonably sure that the student won't track down the reference. But be careful—if the irrelevance is palpable (say you are discussing the evolution of vertebrates and the article you cite is on the evolution of organisms in a completely different phylum or even kingdom), then you may be in trouble if the irrelevancy is pointed out. Make sure the irrelevance is hard to fathom. And then there's the *argument by nonexistent reference*—this works best in public debates.

Because the public debate over evolution tends to pit academic high culture against the burger-eating, Coke-swilling moronic masses, it is helpful to have a technique specifically for keeping the masses in check and the cultural elites suitably sedated. The *argument from aesthetics* answers this call. "This theory is just too beautiful to be false." Evolutionary biologists regularly use this technique to establish the validity of their theories when the evidence for them otherwise is extremely thin.

By now it will be apparent what riches derive from the study of evolutionary logic. We therefore appeal to evolutionary biologists everywhere to institute formal courses in this discipline. This should preferably be done at the undergraduate level so that those who go to teach with only a bachelor's degree will be familiar with the subject. But high school students too should be exposed to the rudiments of evolutionary logic.

It is certain that in the future no one will be able to claim a biological education without a firm grounding in the practical applications of evolutionary logic.[*]

---

[*] This parody adapts and extends Paul Dunmore's "The Uses of Fallacy," *New Zealand Mathematics Magazine*, vol. 7, no. 15, 1970. His article is available online at stuff.mit.edu/people/dpolicar/writing/netsam/logic.html.

NOTES

Foreword

1. Claudia Wallis, "The Evolution Wars," *Time* (August 15, 2005), 26-35.

Chapter 1—Welcome to the Debate

1. Christian Smith, *Soul Searching: The Religious and Spiritual Lives of American Teenagers* (New York: Oxford University Press, 2005), 89.

2. www.clergyletterproject.net.

3. Michael Shermer, *How We Believe: The Search for God in an Age of Science* (New York: Freeman, 2000), 2-3. Excerpt online at www.michaelshermer.com/how-we-believe/excerpt/.

4. His deconversion story is online at www.beliefnet.com/story/172/story_17215_2.html.

5. E.O. Wilson, "Toward a Humanistic Biology," *The Humanist* no. 42, September/October 1982, 40.

6. Gregory W. Graffin and William B. Provine, "Evolution, Religion and Free Will," *American Scientist,* vol. 95, 294. Available online at www.americanscientist.org/template/AssetDetail/assetid/55593.

7. Robert Reich, "The Last Word: Bush's God," *The American Prospect,* June 17, 2004. Available online at www.prospect.org/cs/articles?article=the_last_word_061704 (accessed April 1, 2008).

8. Nancy Pearcey, *Total Truth* (Wheaton, IL: Crossway Books, 2004), 25.

9. Stephen J. Gould, *Ever Since Darwin* (New York: Norton, 1977), 216-17.

10. Charles Darwin, *The Autobiography of Charles Darwin,* ed. N. Barlow (New York: Harcourt Brace, 1959), 92.

11. Dinesh D'Souza, *What's So Great About Christianity* (Washington, DC: Regnery, 2007), 32.

12. David Berlinski, "Darwinism versus Intelligent Design: David Berlinski and Critics," *Commentary,* March 2003, 23.

13. Daniel C. Dennett, *Darwin's Dangerous Idea: Evolution and the Meaning of Life* (New York: Simon & Schuster, 1995), 519.

14. "Council of Europe Makes Its Dogmatism Official: Intelligent Design poses 'a threat to human rights.'" Available online at www.evolutionnews.org/2007/10/council_of_europe_makes_its_do.html.

15. Cited in Roy Abraham Varghese, "The Supreme Science," *Viewpoints,* December 16, 2004, 35A.

16. Antony Flew and Gary Habermas, "My Pilgrimage from Atheism to Theism: A Discussion between Antony Flew and Gary Habermas," *Philosophia Christi,* vol. 6, no. 2, 2004, 201.

17. Antony Flew and Roy Abraham Varghese, *There Is a God: How the World's Most Notorious Atheist Changed His Mind* (New York: HarperOne, 2007), 88.

18. See, for instance, William A. Dembski and Jonathan Wells, *The Design of Life: Discovering Signs of Intelligence in Biological Systems* (Dallas: Foundation for Thought and Ethics, 2008).

19. Richard Dawkins, *The Blind Watchmaker* (New York: Norton, 1986), 1.

20. Francis Crick, *What Mad Pursuit* (New York: Basic Books, 1988), 138.

21. From Judge John E. Jones III's opinion in *Kitzmiller v. Dover,* rendered December 20, 2005. Available online at www.pamd.uscourts.gov/kitzmiller/kitzmiller_342.pdf. (Accessed April 1, 2008.)

22. The successor to that book is Dembski and Wells's *The Design of Life.*

23. For an extended treatment of the errors in *Kitzmiller v. Dover,* see David DeWolf, John West, Casey Luskin, and Jonathan Witt, *Traipsing into Evolution* (Seattle: Discovery Institute, 2006).

24. Ibid., 93-102.

25. Ibid., 9.

Chapter 2—Intelligent Design to the Rescue!

1. Charles Darwin, letter to W. Graham, July 3, 1881, in Francis Darwin, ed., *The Life and Letters of Charles Darwin,* vol. 3 (New York: Basic Books, 1959) 285.

2. Paul Davies, "What Happened Before the Big Bang?" in *God for the 21st Century,* ed. Russell Stannard (Philadelphia: Templeton Foundation Press, 2000), 12.

3. Francis Crick, *The Astonishing Hypothesis: The Scientific Search for the Soul* (New York: Touchstone, 1995), 262.

4. Steve Pinker, *How the Mind Works* (New York: Norton, 1997), 305.

5. *United States v. Seeger,* 380 U.S. 163, 176 (1965). See Francis J. Beckwith, *Law, Darwinism, and Public Education* (Lanham: MD, Rowman & Littlefield, 2003), 146.

6. Aldous Huxley, *Ends and Means: An Inquiry into the Nature of Ideals and into the Methods Employed for Their Realization* (New York: Greenwood, 1969), 273.

7. Rob Lacey, *The Word on the Street* (Grand Rapids: Zondervan, 2004), 357.

8. Peter Carlson, "Billionaires Run Amok on TV?: Satirist Terry Southern's Wacky Idea for Tube a Reality," *Washington Post,* November 12, 2004.

9. Stephen Jay Gould, *Wonderful Life: The Burgess Shale and the Nature of History* (New York: Norton, 1989), 318.

10. "Against Ignorance: Science Education in the 21st Century—A Conversation with Richard Dawkins and Lawrence Krauss," Aurora Forum at Stanford University, March 9, 2008.

11. William Paley, *Natural Theology: Or, Evidences of the Existence and Attributes of the Deity, Collected from the Appearances of Nature* (Boston: Gould and Lincoln, 1852).

12. Francisco J. Ayala, *Darwin's Gift to Science and Religion* (Washington, DC: Joseph Henry Press, 2007), 42.

13. See William Dembski and Jonathan Wells, *The Design of Life* (2008); Michael Behe, *The Edge of Evolution* (2007); Benjamin Wiker and Jonathan Witt, *A Meaningful World* (2006); Jay Richards and Guillermo Gonzalez, *The Privileged Planet* (2004).

14. Mail Call, *Newsweek,* December 20, 2004, 19.

15. Francis J. Beckwith, *Law, Darwinism, and Public Education* (New York: Rowman & Littlefield, 2003), 1.

16. William Dembski, *The Design Inference* (Cambridge: Cambridge University Press, 1998), chs. 2 and 7.

Chapter 3—The Surprising Truth

1. Ernst Mayr, "Darwin's Influence on Modern Thought," *Scientific American* 28, no. 1, 2000, 78-83.

2. Jerry Coyne, "Intelligent Design: The Faith That Dare Not Speak Its Name," in *Intelligent Thought,* ed. by John Brockman (New York: Vintage Books, 2006), 4.

3. Claudia Wallis, "The Evolution Wars," *Time,* August 15, 2005.

4. Michael Ruse, *Darwinism Defended* (Reading, MA: Addison-Wesley, 1982), 58.

5. Francisco J. Ayala, *Darwin's Gift to Science and Religion* (Washington DC: Joseph Henry Press, 2007), 140.

6. Gerald Schroeder, *The Science of God: The Convergence of Scientific and Biblical Wisdom* (New York: Free Press, 1997), 31.

7. Thomas Woodward, *Doubts about Darwin: A History of Intelligent Design* (Grand Rapids: Baker Books, 2003), 197.

8. Adapted from Denyse O'Leary, *By Design or by Chance: The Growing Controversy on the Origins of Life in the Universe* (Minneapolis: Augsburg, 2004), 167-69.

9. Charles Darwin, *On the Origin of Species* (Cambridge, MA: Harvard University Press, 1964), 2.

10. See for example, Michael Denton, *Evolution: A Theory in Crisis* (1986); Richard Milton, *Shattering the Myths of Darwinism* (2000); Michael Behe, *The Edge of Evolution* (2006); William A. Dembski, *Uncommon Dissent: Intellectuals Who Find Darwinism Unconvincing* (2004).

11. Michael Shermer, *Why Darwin Matters: The Case Against Intelligent Design* (New York: Times Books, 2006), 17.

12. Adapted from *The Design of Life: Discovering Signs of Intelligence in Biological Systems* by William A. Dembski and Jonathan Wells (Dallas: Foundation for Thought and Ethics, 2007), 53-54.

13. R. Britten, "Divergence between Samples of Chimpanzee and Human DNA Sequences Is 5%, Counting Indels," *Proceedings of the National Academy of Sciences,* vol. 99, no. 21, October 15, 2002), 13633-35.

14. Dembski and Wells, *The Design of Life,* 9-10.

15. Charles Darwin, letter to Asa Gray, September 10, 1860, in Francis Darwin, ed., *The Life and Letters of Charles Darwin,* vol. 2 (New York: Appleton, 1896), 131.

16. Ayala, *Darwin's Gift to Science and Religion,* 89.

17. Charles Darwin, *On the Origin of Species* (London: John Murray, 1872), 395.

18. Stephen Jay Gould, "Abscheulich! Atrocious!" *Natural History,* March 2000, 42-49.

19. Elizabeth Pennisi, "Haeckel's Embryos: Fraud Rediscovered," *Science,* vol. 277, 1997, 1435.

20. Jonathan Wells, *The Politically Incorrect Guide to Darwinism and Intelligent Design* (Washington, DC: Regnery, 2006), 32.

21. Ibid., 36.

22. Quoted from Elizabeth Pennisi, "Evo-Devo Enthusiasts Get Down to Details," *Science,* vol. 298, November 1, 2002, 953.

23. Coyne, "Intelligent Design," in *Intelligent Thought,* 10.

24. Michael Behe, *The Edge of Evolution* (New York: Free Press, 2006), 15.

25. Ibid., 138-39.

Chapter 4—What Story Do the Rocks Tell?

1. Charles Darwin, *On the Origin of Species* (Cambridge, MA: Harvard University Press, 1964), 189.

2. Ibid., 281-82.

3. Ibid., 280.

4. Ibid.

5. Jonathan Wells, *Icons of Evolution* (Washington, DC, Regnery, 2000), 209-28.

6. Richard Milton, *Shattering the Myths of Darwinism* (Rochester, VA: Park Street Press, 1997), 207.

7. Ibid., 201-2.

8. Ibid., 199-208.

9. The exception is the Ediacaran fauna, a collection of multicelled organisms that went extinct before the Cambrian explosion and that are unrelated to its life forms.

10. Stephen Jay Gould, "Evolution's Erratic Pace," *Natural History,* vol. 86, no. 5, May 1977, 12-16.

11. Darwin, *On the Origin of Species,* 280.

12. From a presentation by Gareth Nelson in 1969 to the American Museum of Natural History, quoted in David M. Williams and Malte C. Ebach, "The Reform of Palaeontology and the Rise of Biogeography—25 Years after 'Ontogeny, Phylogeny, Palaeontology and the Biogenetic Law' (Nelson, 1978)," *Journal of Biogeography,* vol. 31, 2004, 709.

13. Henry Gee, *In Search of Deep Time* (New York: Free Press, 1999), 23, 32, 116-17.

14. S. Iyengar and J. Greenhouse, "Selection Models and the File Drawer Problem (with Discussion)," *Statistical Science,* vol. 3, 1988, 109-35.

15. Tim Berra, *Evolution and the Myth of Creationism* (Stanford, CA: Stanford University Press, 1990), 117-19.

16. Stephen Meyer, "The Cambrian Information Explosion," in *Debating Design,* ed. by William A. Dembski and Michael Ruse (New York: Cambridge University Press, 2006), 378.

17. Ibid.

Chapter 5—Science or Religion?

1. Ross Clifford, *Leading Lawyers' Case for the Resurrection* (Edmonton, AB: Canadian Institute for Law, Theology and Public Policy, 1996), 104-5.

2. Alvin Plantinga, "Methodological Naturalism?" from *Perspectives on Science and Christian Faith,* vol. 49, September 1997, 143-54. Available online at www.asa3.org/ASA/topics/Philosophy/PSCF9-97Plantinga.html (accessed Oct 12, 2007).

3. Francisco J. Ayala, "Darwin's Revolution," in *Creative Evolution?!,* ed. by J.H. Campbell and J.W. Schopf (Boston: Jones and Bartlett, 1994), 4.

4. David Hull, *Darwin and His Critics: The Reception of Darwin's Theory of Evolution by the Scientific Community* (Cambridge, MA: Harvard University Press, 1973), 26.

5. Richard Dawkins, *The God Delusion* (London: Bantam Books, 2006), 58-59.

6. William Dembski and Jonathan Wells, *The Design of Life: Discovering Signs of Intelligence in Biological Systems* (Dallas: Foundation for Thought and Ethics, 2008); Guillermo Gonzalez and Jay W. Richards, *The Privileged Planet: How Our Place in the Cosmos Is Designed for Discovery* (Washington, DC: Regnery, 2004).

7. Eugenie Scott, "'Science and Religion,' 'Christian Scholarship,' and 'Theistic Science': Some Comparisons," *Reports of the National Center for Science Education,* vol. 18, no. 2, 1998, 30-32. Available online at www.ncseweb.org/resources/articles/6149_science_and_religion_chris_3_1_1998.asp (accessed March 18, 2008).

8. J.P. Moreland, *Kingdom Triangle* (Grand Rapids: Zondervan, 2007), 41.

9. Geoffrey Cowley, "The Science of Happiness," *Newsweek,* September 16, 2002, 46.

10. Richard Dawkins, Book Review, *New York Times,* April 9, 1989.

11. Inside Science News Service, "Physics Nobelist takes stand on evolution," American Institute of Physics. Available online at *www.aip.org/isns/reports/2003/081.html* (accessed October 2007).

12. Thomas Clark and Colin Stearn, *Geological Evolution of North America: A Regional Approach to Historical Geology* (New York: Ronald Press, 1960), 43.

13. Michael Crichton, "Aliens Cause Global Warming," Caltech Michelin Lecture, January 17, 2003. Available online at www.crichton-official.com/speech-alienscauseglobalwarming.html (accessed March 18, 2008).

14. Michael Shermer, *Why Darwin Matters: The Case Against Intelligent Design* (New York: Times Books, 2006), 99.

15. Mary Carmichael, "A Changing Portrait of DNA," *Newsweek*, December 10, 2007, 64.

16. See Richard Weikart, *From Darwin to Hitler* (New York: Palgrave Macmillan, 2004).

17. Jonathan Wells, *The Politically Incorrect Guide to Darwinism and Intelligent Design* (Washington DC: Regnery, 2006), 164.

18. "Free People from Superstition," interview with Steven Weinberg, *Free Thought Today*, April 2004. Available online at ffrf.org/fttoday/2000/april2000/weinberg.html (accessed March 18, 2008).

19. James Shapiro, "In the Details…What?" Review of Michael Behe's *Darwin's Black Box*. *National Review*, September 16, 1996, 62-65.

20. David Depew, "Intelligent Design and Irreducible Complexity: A Rejoinder," in *Darwinism, Design, and Public Education*, ed. by Stephen C. Meyer (East Lansing, MI: Michigan State Press, 2003), 447.

Chapter 6—The Design Inference

1. William A. Dembski, *The Design Inference: Eliminating Chance Through Small Probabilities* (Cambridge: Cambridge University Press, 1998).

2. Perhaps that luck will change given that the SETI research lab at UC Berkeley has now received a $25 million donation from Paul Allen, the cofounder of Microsoft. See "Allen Telescope Array Begins Scientific Observations" at www.seti.org/ata/ (accessed on March 27, 2008).

3. See Peter S. Williams, "The Design Inference from Specified Complexity Defended by Scholars Outside the Intelligent Design Movement: A Critical Review," *Philosophia Christi*, vol. 9, no. 2, 2007, 407-28.

4. Dembski, *The Design Inference*, 19, 36.

5. The version of the Explanatory Filter we use here is from William A. Dembski, *The Design Revolution* (Downers Grove, IL: InterVarsity, 2004), 88.

6. Richard Dawkins, *The Blind Watchmaker: Why the Evidence of Evolution Reveals a Universe Without Design* (New York: Norton, 1986), 47.

7. Ibid., 49.

8. William A. Dembski and Jonathan Wells, *The Design of Life: Discovering Signs of Intelligence in Biological Systems* (Dallas: Foundation for Thought and Ethics, 2008), 178-79.

9. See Seth Lloyd, "Computational Capacity of the Universe," *Physical Review Letters*, vol. 88, no. 23, 2002, 7901-4. For a popularization of this work, see Seth Lloyd, *Programming the Universe: A Quantum Computer Scientist Takes on the Cosmos* (New York: Knopf, 2006).

10. Antony Flew, *There Is a God: How the World's Most Notorious Atheist Changed His Mind* (New York: HarperOne, 2007), 77-78.

11. "Monkey Tempest Type Test," *Sky News*, May 9, 2003. Available online at news.sky.com/skynews/article/0,,31500-12310228,00.html (accessed March 27, 2008). Also see David

Adam, "Give six monkeys a computer, and what do you get? Certainly not the Bard" by David Adam in *The Guardian,* May 9, 2003. Available online at: www.guardian.co.uk/uk_news/story/0,3604,952227,00.html (accessed March 27, 2008).

12. Dembski, *The Design Revolution,* 145.

13. Holmes Rolston III, *Genes, Genesis and God: Values and Their Origins in Natural and Human History* (New York: Cambridge University Press, 1999), 352.

Chapter 7—An Unsolved Mystery: The Origin of Life

1. George M. Whitesides, "Revolutions in Chemistry," *Chemical & Engineering News,* vol. 85, no. 13, March 26, 2007, 12-17. Available online at pubs.acs.org/cen/coverstory/85/8513cover1.html (accessed march 27, 2008).

2. Franklin Harold, *The Way of the Cell: Molecules, Organisms, and the Order of Life* (New York: Oxford University Press, 2001), 235.

3. Andy Knoll, PBS *Nova* interview, May 3, 2004.

4. Charles Darwin, in Francis Darwin, ed., *The Life and Letters of Charles Darwin,* vol. 3 (London: John Murray, 1888), 18.

5. Robert Shapiro, *Origins: A Skeptic's Guide to the Origin of Life* (New York: Summit, 1986), 185.

6. Richard Dawkins, *The Blind Watchmaker: Why the Evidence of Evolution Reveals a Universe without Design* (New York: Norton, 1987), 6.

7. Ernst Haeckel, *The Wonders of Life,* trans. by J. McCabe (London: Watts, 1905), 111.

8. Francis Crick, *Life Itself: Its Origin and Nature* (New York: Simon & Schuster, 1981), 70-71.

9. See William A. Dembski and Jonathan Wells, *The Design of Life: Discovering Signs of Itelligence in Biological Systems* (Dallas: Foundation for Thought and Ethics, 2008), chapter 8.

10. Michael Denton, *Evolution: A Theory in Crisis* (Chevy Chase, MD: Adler and Adler, 1986), 264.

11. Cited in Robert Shapiro, *Origins* (New York: Summit, 1986), 99.

12. J.H. Carver, "Prebiotic Atmospheric Oxygen Levels," *Nature,* vol. 292, 1981, 136-38; James F. Kasting, "Earth's Early Atmosphere," *Science,* vol. 259, 1993, 920-26.

13. Jon Cohen, "Novel Center Seeks to Add Spark to Origins of Life," *Science,* vol. 270, 1995, 1925-26.

14. Massimo Pigliucci, "Where Do We Come From?" in *Darwin, Design and Public Education,* ed. by Stephen Myer and John Campbell (East Lansing, MI: Michigan State Press, 2003), 196.

15. Stephen C. Meyer, "The Origin of Life and the Death of Materialsim." *The Intercollegiate Review,* vol. 31, no. 2, 1996, 24-23. Available online at www.mmisi.org/ir/31_02/meyer.pdf. (accessed April 1, 2008).

16. *Unlocking the Mystery of Life,* Illustra Media, 2002. The DVD is available at www.illustramedia.com.

17. Peter B. Medawar, *Advice to Young Scientists* (New York: HarperCollins, 1981), 39. Emphasis in the original.

18. Quoted in Robert Irion, "RNA Can't Take the Heat," *Science,* vol. 279, 1998, 1303.

19. Stuart Kauffman, *At Home in the Universe* (New York: Oxford University Press, 1995), 31.

20. Francis S. Collins, "Faith and the Human Genome," *Perspectives on Science and Christian Faith,* vol. 55, no. 3, 2003, 152.

21. G.C. Williams, "A Package of Information" in J. Brockman, ed., *The Third Culture: Beyond the Scientific Revolution* (New York: Simon & Schuster, 1995), 43. Available online at www.edge.org/documents/ThirdCulture/h-Ch.1.html.

22. Jacob D. Bekenstein, "Information in the Holographic Universe," *Scientific American,* July 14, 2003. Available online at www.sciam.com/print_version. cfm?articleID=000AF072-4891-1F0A-97AE80A84189EEDF.

23. The information in this sidebar is adapted from Denyse O'Leary, *By Design or by Chance?: The Growing Controversy on the Origins of Life in the Universe* (Minneapolis: Augsburg Fortress, 2004), 233-34.

24. Denton, *Evolution,* 334.

25. Bill Gates, *The Road Ahead* (Boulder, CO: Blue Penguin, 1996), 228.

26. Stephen C. Meyer, "DNA and the Origin of Life," in *Darwinism, Design, and Public Education,* ed. by Stephen C. Meyer (East Lansing, MI: Michigan State Press, 2003), 229.

27. Antony Flew and Roy Abraham Varghese, *There Is a God: How the World's Most Notorious Atheist Changed His Mind* (New York: HarperOne, 2007), 132.

Chapter 8—Putting Darwin's Theory to the Test

1. Charles Darwin, *On the Origin of Species* (Cambridge, MA: Harvard University Press, 1964), 189. Although this test seems to make a far-reaching concession, it actually imposes conditions that cannot be met. In reality, the test is no test at all. For how could someone investigate every conceivable naturalistic pathway for the origin of a complex organ and show that it fails? Darwin was shifting the burden of proof to those who doubt his theory. So as a result, he didn't have to offer any detailed, plausible accounts of the origin of complex organisms.

2. Ibid., 194.

3. See note 1 above.

4. Michael Behe, "Irreducible Complexity: Obstacle to Darwinian Evolution," in *Debating Design,* ed. by William A. Dembski and Michael Ruse (New York: Cambridge University Press, 2004), 353.

5. H. Allen Orr, "Darwin v. Intelligent Design (Again)," *Boston Review,* December/January 1996-1997, 29.

6. See L. Nguyen, I.T. Paulsen, J. Tchieu, C.J. Hueck, M.H. Saier Jr., "Phylogenetic Analyses of the Constituents of Type III Protein Secretion Systems," *Journal of Molecular Microbiology and Biotechnology,* vol. 2, no. 2, 2000, 125-44.

7. Lynn Margulis and Dorion Sagan, *Acquiring Genomes: A Theory of the Origins of Species* (New York: Basic Books, 2002), 103.

8. Franklin Harold, *The Way of the Cell: Molecules, Organisms and the Order of Life* (Oxford: Oxford University Press, 2001), 205; James Shapiro, "In the Details...What?" *National Review,* September 16, 1996, 62-65.

9. See Behe's numerous responses to critics at www.discovery.org/csc/fellows.php (click on his name and then "articles") as well as his online blog at www.amazon.com.

10. Michael Behe, *Darwin's Black Box: The Biochemical Challenge to Evolution* (New York: Free Press, 2006), 266.

11. Michael J. Behe, *The Edge of Evolution: The Search for the Limits of Darwinism* (New York: Free Press, 2007), 15-16.

Chapter 9—At Home in the Universe

1. Freeman J. Dyson, *Disturbing the Universe* (New York: Harper & Row, 1979), 250.

2. Quoted in Henry Margenau and Roy Varghese, eds., *Cosmos, Bios, and Theos* (LaSalle, IL: Open Court, 1992), 83.

3. Quoted in Paul Davies, *The Accidental Universe* (Cambridge: Cambridge University Press, 1982), 118.

4. Paul Davies, *Superforce: The Search for a Grand Unified Theory of Nature* (New York: Simon & Schuster, 1984), 242.

5. Walter L. Bradley, "The 'Just So' Universe," in *Signs of Intelligence,* ed. by William A. Dembski and James M. Kushiner (Grand Rapids, MI: Brazos Press, 2001), 169.

6. Roger Penrose, *The Emperor's New Mind* (New York: Oxford, 1989), 344.

7. Paul Davies, *Cosmic Jackpot* (New York: Houghton Mifflin, 2007), 149.

8. Ibid., 2-3.

9. Antony Flew, *There Is a God: How the World's Most Notorious Atheist Changed His Mind* (New York: HarperOne, 2007), 119.

10. Robin Collins, "A Scientific Argument for the Existence of God," in *Reason for the Hope Within* (Grand Rapids: Eerdmans, 1999), 55.

11. Lee Smolin, *The Life of the Cosmos* (New York: Oxford University Press, 1997), 24. Quoted in Dinesh D'Souza, *What's So Great About Christianity* (Washington DC: Regnery, 2007), 133.

12. Frederick Hoyle, *The Intelligent Universe* (London: Michael Joseph, 1983), 220.

13. John Leslie, "How to Draw Conclusions from a Fine-Tuned Cosmos" in R.J. Russell, W.R. Stoeger, and G.V. Coyne, eds., *Physics, Philosophy and Theology: A Common Quest for Understanding* (Vatican City: Vatican Observatory Press, 1988), 304.

14. Davies, *Cosmic Jackpot,* 138.

15. Flew, *There Is a God,* 137.

16. Ibid., 121.

17. See www.youtube.com/watch?v=JWVshkVF0SY (accessed on March 31, 2008).

18. Carl Sagan, *Pale Blue Dot: A Vision of the Human Future in Space* (New York: Ballantine Books, 1994), 7.

19. Victor Stenger, *God: The Failed Hypothesis* (Amherst, NY: Prometheus Books, 2007), 161.

20. Blaise Pascal, *Pensées,* no. 348, trans. by W.F. Trotter, in R.M. Hutchins, ed., *Great Books of the Western World* (Chicago: Encyclopedia Britannica, 1952), 234.

21. Julian of Norwich, *Showings,* ed. and trans. by E. College and J. Walsh, Classics of Western Spirituality (New York: Paulist Press, 1988), 131-32.

22. G.K. Chesterton, *Orthodoxy,* in *Collected Works of G. K. Chesterton,* vol. 1 (San Francisco: Ignatius, 1986), 264-65.

23. Guillermo Gonzalez and Jay W. Richards, *The Privileged Planet* (Washington, DC, Regnery, 2004).

24. Ibid., 152.

25. Larry Chapman, Rick James, and Eric Stanford, "What are the Odds?" in *Y-Origins,* 2004, 21.

26. See Donald Brownlee and Peter D. Ward, *Rare Earth: Why Complex Life Is Uncommon in the Universe* (New York: Springer, 2003).

27. Gonzalez and Richards, *The Privileged Planet,* xv.

28. Quoted in Lee Strobel, *The Case for a Creator* (Grand Rapids: Zondervan, 2004), 189.

29. Psalm 19:1-2 NIV.

30. See Dinesh D'Souza *What's So Great About Christianity* (Washington, DC: Regnery, 2007), 119.

31. Quoted in Malcolm Browne, "Clues to the Universe's Origin Expected," *New York Times*, March 12, 1978.

32. Thomas Woodward, *Darwin Strikes Back* (Grand Rapids, MI: Baker Books, 2006), 157.

33. From our perspective, the beginning of space, time, and matter itself requires an out-of-time eternal source for its existence. William Lane Craig and J.P. Moreland defend this view in *Philosophical Foundations for a Christian Worldview* (Downers Grove, IL: Inter-Varsity Press, 2003), chapter 23. Bertrand Russell, on the other hand, famously argued that we still need to answer the question, "Who made God?" See Bertrand Russell, *Why I am Not a Christian* (New York: Simon & Schuster, 1957).

34. Robert Jastrow, *God and the Astronomers* (New York: Norton, 2000), 107.

Chapter 10—Joining the Design Revolution

1. Thomas Woodward, *Darwin Strikes Back: Defending Intelligent Design* (Grand Rapids: Baker Books, 2006), 175-76.

2. Jonathan Wells, *The Politically Incorrect Guide to Darwinism and Intelligent Design* (Washington, DC: Regnery, 2006), 195.

3. Earlier draft of Edward Sisson, "Teaching the Flaws in Neo-Darwinism," in William A. Dembski, ed., *Uncommon Dissent: Intellectuals Who Find Darwinism Unconvincing* (Wilmington, DE: ISI Books, 2004), 88.

4. Adapted from Edward Sisson, "Teaching the Flaws in Neo-Darwinism," 87-89.

5. Quoted in interview with Fiona Morgan, "Louisiana calls Darwin a racist," Salon, May 4, 2001. Available online at archive.salon.com/news/feature/2001/05/04/darwin/print. html (accessed March 24, 2008).

6. See David DeWolf, John West, Casey Luskin, and Jonathan Witt, *Traipsing into Evolution: Intelligent Design and the Kitzmiller v. Dover Decision* (Seattle: Discovery Institute Press, 2006).

7. Richard Halvorson, "Questioning the Orthodoxy: Intelligent Design Theory Is Breaking the Scientific Monopoly of Darwinism," *Harvard Political Review*, May 14, 2002.

8. Richard Halverson wrote this op-ed as a senior at Harvard. It appeared April 7, 2003 in the *Harvard Crimson*. Available online at www.thecrimson.com/article. aspx?ref=347399 (access March 24, 2008). Used by permission.

9. Francisco Ayala, *Darwin's Gift to Science and Religion* (Washington, DC: Joseph Henry Press, 2007), 159-60.

10. *Catholic Encyclopedia*, s.v. "Evil." Available online at www.newadvent.org/cathen/05649a.htm (accessed March 15, 2007). In support of this passage, the *Catholic Encyclopedia* cites Dionysius the Areopagite and Augustine.

11. Our thanks to Casey Luskin, head of the IDEA Club Chapter program, for his help on these action points.

Index

It's a Harsh,

Crazy,

Beautiful,

Messed Up,

Breathtaking

World...

And People Are Talking About It...

conversant life.com

engage your faith